T0363828

STORYFUN 6

TEACHER'S BOOK

Second edition

Karen Saxby
Emily Hird

Cambridge University Press

www.cambridge.org/elt

Cambridge English Language Assessment

www.cambridgeenglish.org

Information on this title: www.cambridge.org/9781316617298

© Cambridge University Press and UCLES 2017

First published 2011 © Cambridge University Press
Second edition 2017 © Cambridge University Press and UCLES

20 19 18 17 16 15 14 13 12 11 10 9 8 7 6

Printed in Great Britain by CPI Group (UK) Ltd, Croydon CR0 4YY

A catalogue record for this publication is available from the British Library

ISBN 978-1-316-61725-0 Student's Book with online activities and Home Fun booklet 6
ISBN 978-1-316-61729-8 Teacher's Book with Audio 6
ISBN 978-1-316-61733-5 Presentation plus 6

The publishers have no responsibility for the persistence or accuracy of URLs for external or third-party internet websites referred to in this publication, and do not guarantee that any content on such websites is, or will remain, accurate or appropriate. Information regarding prices, travel timetables, and other factual information given in this work is correct at the time of first printing but the publishers do not guarantee the accuracy of such information thereafter.

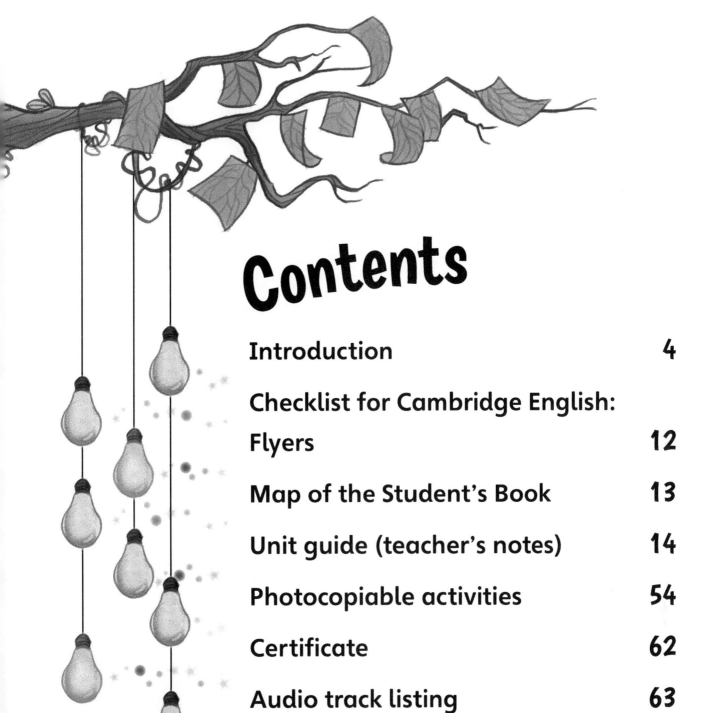

Contents

☆ = Value

♪ = Song

✔ = Test tasks for Flyers

➡ = Practice for Flyers

✳ = Let's have fun! pages

💬 = Let's speak! pages

🔊 = Let's say! pages

▶ = Audio

IA = Interactive activity

🏠 = Home FUN booklet

👆 = Online activities

Introduction

Welcome to *Storyfun*!

Storyfun is a series of six books written for young learners aged between 6 and 12 years. The series provides story-based preparation for the Cambridge English: Young Learners tests (YLE). Each Student's Book contains eight stories with activities that include vocabulary and grammar tasks, puzzles, games, poems, songs and an exploration of the story 'value' (for example, an appreciation of nature, the importance of friendship). The Teacher's Books provide detailed suggestions on how to approach the storytelling, together with clear instructions for guiding learners through the unit. With a variety of flexible resources, each unit in *Storyfun* is designed to provide approximately three to four hours of class time.

Why stories?

Storyfun aims to provide an opportunity for language practice by engaging learners' interest in stories.

Research has shown that meaningful and imaginative stories can motivate learning because learners:

o   engage with the text and their imaginations.
o   learn vocabulary with repetition of key words in the text and pictures.
o   are exposed to repeated rhyme and sound patterns and accurate pronunciation.
o   develop deeper social understanding by relating to characters and events in the story.
o   actively engage listening skills as they predict, hypothesise and await outcomes.

Points to remember for effective learning:

o   Story-reading should be interactive (teacher and learners). It should involve pointing, describing and discussing how the story relates to the real world.
o   Learners will engage with a story more if they are encouraged to 'work out' the meaning, for example, why learners think characters did something or how characters felt at a certain moment and, of course, what the story 'value' is.
o   Learners benefit from more than one reading or hearing of a story. At least one reading should be read/heard right the way through from beginning to end without interruption.

For more information about stories in language learning, go to

Why Cambridge English: Young Learners (YLE)?

The stories have been written to reflect the different language levels and topic areas of the Cambridge English: Starters, Movers and Flyers tests and to appeal to the target-reader age groups. The language of the stories is exploited in activities that check comprehension, teach key vocabulary and grammar, practise all four language skills (reading, writing, listening and speaking) and give learners an opportunity to familiarise themselves with

the nature and format of the Cambridge English: Young Learners tests. The optional *Let's have fun!* and *Let's speak!* sections at the back of the books also provide opportunities for collaborative learning and test speaking practice. The *Let's say!* pages support early pronunciation skills, building from sounds to sentences.

There are two Student's Books for each test: pre-A1 (Starters), A1 (Movers) and A2 (Flyers). *Storyfun 5* gently introduces students to the Cambridge English: Flyers language and topics through fun activities and test-style practice. Activities are carefully graded to ensure learners are guided towards the test level, with frequent opportunities to build up their language and skills. *Storyfun 6* provides examples of all the Cambridge English: Flyers test tasks. By the end of *Storyfun* levels 5 and 6, constant recycling of language and test task types ensures learners are fully prepared for the Cambridge English: Flyers test.

Who is *Storyfun* for?

Storyfun has been written for teachers and young learners of English in a wide variety of situations. It is suitable for:

o   learners in this age group who enjoy reading and listening to stories
o   large and small groups of learners
o   monolingual and multilingual classes
o   learners who are beginning preparation for the Cambridge English: Young Learners tests
o   young learners who need to develop their vocabulary, grammar and language
o   young learners keen to discuss social values, develop collaborative learning skills and build confidence for the Speaking papers
o   teachers who wish to develop their learners' literacy skills

What are the key features of *Storyfun 6*?

Student's Book

o   eight imaginative and motivating stories
o   fun, interactive, creative and meaningful activities
o   activities similar to task types found in all three parts (Reading and Writing, Listening and Speaking) of the Cambridge English: Flyers test

- o an introduction to Cambridge English: Flyers grammar and vocabulary
- o extension activities *Let's have fun!*, further speaking practice *Let's speak!* and an early pronunciation focus *Let's say!*
- o a unit-by-unit word list

Home FUN booklet

- o fun activities for learners to try at home
- o 'self-assessment' activities that build learners' confidence and encourage autonomy
- o a Cambridge English: Flyers picture dictionary
- o *Let's have fun!* pages to encourage learners to use English in the wider world
- o answers, audio and additional support found online by using the access code at the front of the book

Teacher's Book with Audio

- o a map of the Student's Book (topics, grammar points and Flyers test practice for each unit)
- o practical step-by-step notes with suggestions for:

  - ✓ personalisation at presentation and practice stages
  - ✓ skills work: reading, writing, listening, speaking, drawing and colouring
  - ✓ pair and group work
  - ✓ puzzles, games, poems and songs
  - ✓ speaking activities and projects
  - ✓ discussion tasks to explore the story 'value'
  - ✓ recycling of language
  - ✓ incorporating digital materials into the lesson

- o Cambridge English: Flyers test tips
- o full audioscripts
- o imaginative audio recordings for stories and activities (downloadable by using the access code at the front of this book) reflective of the Cambridge English: Flyers Listening test
- o photocopiable pages for the Student's Book or optional extension activities
- o links to online practice and the Home FUN booklet

Presentation plus

- o digital version of all Student's Book pages
- o interactive Student's Book activities
- o audio played directly from the digital page
- o digital flashcards with audio
- o digital slideshow of every story
- o an Image carousel that provides further visuals associated with story themes
- o integrated tools to make notes and highlight activities

Online practice

For the Teacher
- o Presentation plus
- o All audio recordings
- o Additional digital resources to support your classes

For the Student
- o Fun activities to practise the exam, skills and language
- o All audio recordings
- o Additional digital resources

Word FUN World app

- o Cambridge English: Young Learners vocabulary game
- o For mobile phones and tablets

Storytelling

Why should we use stories in language learning classes?

There are several reasons! A good story encourages us to turn the next page and read more. We want to find out what happens next and what the main characters do and say to each other. We may feel excited, sad, afraid, angry or really happy. The experience of reading or listening to a story is likely to make us 'feel' that we are part of the story, too. Just like in our 'real' lives, we might love or hate different characters. Perhaps we recognise ourselves or other people we know in some of the story characters. Perhaps they have similar talents, ambitions, weaknesses or problems.

Because of this natural connection with story characters, our brains process the reading of stories differently from the way we read factual information. This is because our brains don't always recognise the difference between an imagined situation and a real one so the characters become 'alive' to us. What they say or do is therefore <u>much more meaningful</u>. The words and structures that relate a story's events, descriptions and conversations are processed by learners in a deeper way.

Encouraging learners to read or listen to stories should therefore help them to learn a second language in a way that is not only fun, but memorable.

How else do stories help?

Stories don't only offer the young reader a chance to learn more vocabulary and develop their grammatical skills. The experience also creates an opportunity to develop critical and creative thinking, emotional literacy and social skills. As learners read a story, they will be imagining far more details than its words communicate. Each learner will, subconsciously, be 'animating' the characters and making judgements and predictions about events.

As a teacher, you can encourage creativity and critical thinking by asking learners in groups to develop characters in more detail, talk about the part of the story they enjoyed most/least or even write different endings. You can also discuss, in English or L1 if necessary, the story 'values'; in other words, what different stories teach us about how to relate to others.

Stories also offer a forum for personalised learning. No two learners will feel exactly the same about a story and an acceptance of difference can also be interesting to explore and discuss in class.

How can we encourage learners to join in and ask parents to help?

If, at first, learners lack confidence or motivation to read stories in English, help by reading the story to them without stopping so learners are just enjoying the story, stress free, and following as well as they can by looking at the pictures. During a second reading you might encourage interaction by asking questions like *Is this funny, scary or sad?* (Starters) *Was that a good idea?* (Movers) *What do you think will happen next?* (Flyers). If the class is read to in a relaxed and fun way, learners will subconsciously relate to the reading and language learning process more confidently and positively. Of course, being read to by a parent at home, too, is also simply a lovely way to share quiet and close time. To engage parents in the language learning process, you might share some of the above points with them or encourage them to search online for language learning activities to do at home with their children.

The Home FUN booklet has been specially designed for learners to use at home with parents. Activities are fun and easy to follow, requiring little instruction. The booklet aims to help learners show parents what they have learnt at school and to engage them in the learning process.

Further suggestions for storytelling

o   Involve learners in the topic and ask guessing and prediction questions in L1 if necessary. This will engage learners in the process of storytelling and motivate learning. When you pause the audio during the story, ask learners:

  ➢   about the topic and themselves
  ➢   to guess aspects of the story
  ➢   to say how they think a character feels or what they may say next

o   If you are telling the story yourself, support your learners in any way you can by adding your own dramatisation. For instance, you can read the stories with as much animation as possible and use props such as puppets or soft toys and different voices to bring the stories to life.

o   Incorporate the use of realia into the storytelling process. For example, if you are using *Storyfun 6*, in 'A cake for a queen' you could take in some cooking utensils, and in 'Katy's favourite song' you could take in a guitar and a microphone.

o   Once learners are familiar with the story they could even act out parts of the story in role plays. This will not only involve learners in the stories and add a fun element but can also help in practising and consolidating language.

Suggestions for using the story pictures

For skills practice

o   Before listening to the story, learners look at all the pictures on the story pages and discuss in small groups who or what they think the story is about and what the key events are.

o   Learners trace a picture (adding their own choice of extra details) and then follow your colouring or drawing instructions.

To encourage creative thinking

o   Groups choose two people in a picture and imagine what they are saying to each other. They then write a question with answer or a short dialogue.

o   Groups choose a background person in a picture and invent details about him/her. For example, how old they are, what they like doing, where they live, what pet they have.

o   Groups invent details that are unseen in the picture, for example, ten things in a bag, cupboard or garden.

o   Learners imagine they are 'in' the picture. What is behind / in front of / next to them? What can they feel (the sun, a cold wind …), smell (flowers, cooking …) or hear (birds, traffic …)?

To revise vocabulary and grammar

- Learners find as many things in a picture as they can which begin with a particular letter, for example, *f*.
- Learners list things in a picture that are a certain colour or in a certain place. For example, what someone is wearing or what is on the table.
- Learners choose four things they can see in a picture and list the words according to the size of the object or length of the word. Learners could also choose things according to categories such as food or animals.
- Use the pictures to revise grammar, for example *This is / These are*.
- Choose a picture in the story and ask learners in groups to say what is happening in this part of the story.
- Practise prepositions by asking learners what they can see in a picture in different places, for example, in the box, on the table or under the tree.
- Practise question forms by asking learners about different aspects of a picture, for example: *What colour is the cat? How many ducks are there? What's the boy doing?*
- On the board, write the first and last letter of four things learners can remember in a particular story picture. Learners complete the words.
- Point to objects or people in a picture and ask *This/These yes/no* questions. For example: *Is this a shoe? Are these toys? Is this a boy? Are these hats?*
- Ask *yes/no* colour and *how many* questions. For example, point to an apple and ask *Is this apple blue? Can you see four apples?*
- Show learners a story picture for 30 seconds and then ask *What's in that picture?* Write learners' answers on the board.
- Ask simple *What's the word* questions and build on known vocabulary sets. For example: *It's green. You can eat it. It's a fruit.* (a pear / an apple / a grape / a kiwi)

Suggestions for using the word list

At the back of the Student's Book, learners will find a list of important Flyers words that appear in each unit.

- Play 'Which word am I?' Learners work in pairs, looking at the word list for the unit. Choose a noun and give the class clues about it until one pair guesses it. Don't make the clues too easy and focus on form first and meaning afterwards. Say, for example: *I've got four letters. The letter 'k' is in me. You can sit on me. You can ride me to school.* (bike)
- Divide the class into A and B pairs. Learner A sits facing the board. Learner B sits with his/her back to the board. Write four words (nouns or verbs are best) from the word list for the unit on the board. Learner A then draws or mimes them until their partner guesses them all and writes them correctly (with the help of Learner A who can only say *Yes, that's right!* or *No, that's wrong!*). When everyone has finished, learners change places. Write some new words on the board. Learner B in each pair mimes these words for Learner A to guess.
- Play 'Tell me more, please!' Choose a noun from the word list for the unit and write it on the board, for example: *banana*. Learners take turns to add more information about the banana. For example, Learner A says: *The banana is long.* Learner B adds: *The banana is long. It's yellow.* Learner C says: *The banana is long. It's yellow. It's a fruit.* Continue until learners can't remember previous information.

- Pairs work together to make as many words from the word list for the unit as they can, using a number of letters that you dictate to the class. Alternatively, use word tiles from board games or letter cards made by the class. These could also be used for spelling tests in pairs or groups.
- On the board, write eight words from the word list for the unit with the letters jumbled. Pairs work as fast as they can to find the words and spell them correctly.
- On the board, write eight words from the word list for the unit. Spell three or four of them incorrectly. Pairs work as fast as they can to identify the misspelt words (they shouldn't be told how many there are) and to write them down correctly.
- Play 'Make a word'. Each group chooses a word (four, five or six letters long) from the word list for the unit and creates it by forming a human sculpture, i.e. learners in each group stand in a line, using their arms or legs to create the shapes of each letter. Remember you may need two learners for some letters (e.g. *k*). When all the groups are ready, the words are guessed.
- Use the word list for the unit to play common word games such as hangman, bingo and definition games or for dictated spelling tests. A nice alternative to the traditional hangman, which learners may enjoy, is an animal with its mouth open, with 8–10 steps leading down into its mouth. (You could use a crocodile at Starters, a shark at Movers or a dinosaur at Flyers.) With each incorrect guess, the stick person falls down onto the next step, and gets eaten if they reach the animal's mouth!

For more information on Cambridge English: Young Learners, please visit. From here, you can download the handbook for teachers, which includes information about each level of the Young Learners tests. You can also find information for candidates and their parents, including links to videos of the Speaking test at each level. There are also sample test papers, as well as further games and songs and links to the Teaching Support website.

A few final classroom points

Please try to be as encouraging as possible when working through the activities. By using phrases such as *Now you! You choose! Well done! Don't worry!* you are also helping learners to feel more confident about participating fully in the class and trying hard to do their best. Make sure that everyone in your class adds to open class work, however minimally, and when mistakes are made, view them as opportunities for learning. Try not to interrupt to correct learners during open class discussion, role plays, etc. Doing so might negatively affect a child's willingness to contribute in future. It takes courage to speak out in class. Make mental notes of mistakes and then cover them at a later moment with the whole class.

Have fun!

But most of all, please remember that an hour's lesson can feel very much longer than that to a learner who feels excluded, fearful of making mistakes, unsure about what to do, unable to follow instructions or express any personal opinions. An hour's lesson will feel like five minutes if a learner is having fun, sensing their own progress and participating fully in enjoyable and meaningful activities.

How is the Student's Book organised?

Story

Four illustrated story pages using language (topics, vocabulary and grammar) needed for the Cambridge English: Flyers test.

Vocabulary activity

Each unit of four-page activities opens with a vocabulary comprehension activity related to the key Cambridge English: Flyers vocabulary presented in the story.

Value

Each story explores a 'value'. For example, the value in Unit 1 is *Learning to be independent*. In some units, a key English phrase within the story demonstrates the story value. For example, in Unit 4, *Showing kindness* ➜ "This is for you!"

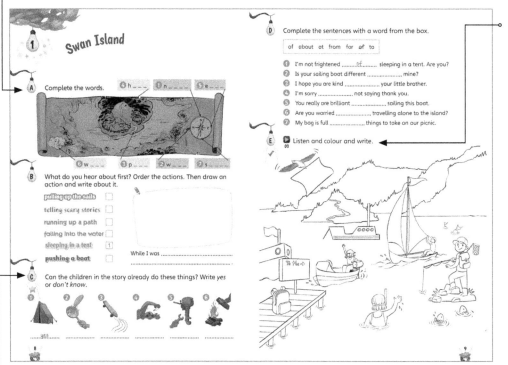

✔ Test tasks for Flyers

Authentic activities that follow the exact format of Cambridge English: Flyers test tasks.

➡ Practice for Flyers

Specific activities that gently build up learners' familiarity and practise for the Cambridge English: Flyers test.

☆ Value activities

encourage learners to think about the story in a social context.

Skills

All activities develop reading, writing, listening and speaking skills useful for the YLE tests.

Songs

Open activities such as poems and songs maintain learners' motivation and interest.

Let's have fun!

Optional projects or games at the back of the Student's Book promote collaborative learning.

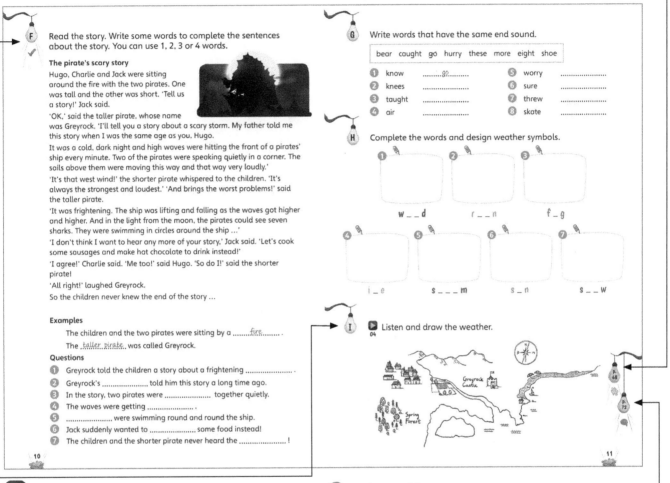

F Read the story. Write some words to complete the sentences about the story. You can use 1, 2, 3 or 4 words.

The pirate's scary story

Hugo, Charlie and Jack were sitting around the fire with the two pirates. One was tall and the other was short. 'Tell us a story!' Jack said.

'OK,' said the taller pirate, whose name was Greyrock. 'I'll tell you a story about a scary storm. My father told me this story when I was the same age as you, Hugo.

It was a cold, dark night and high waves were hitting the front of a pirate's ship every minute. Two of the pirates were speaking quietly in a corner. The sails above them were moving this way and that way very loudly.'

'It's that west wind!' the shorter pirate whispered to the children. 'It's always the strongest and loudest.' 'And brings the worst problems!' said the taller pirate.

'It was frightening. The ship was lifting and falling as the waves got higher and higher. And in the light from the moon, the pirates could see seven sharks. They were swimming in circles around the ship ...'

'I don't think I want to hear any more of your story,' Jack said. 'Let's cook some sausages and make hot chocolate to drink instead!'

'I agree!' Charlie said. 'Me too!' said Hugo. 'So do I!' said the shorter pirate!

'All right!' laughed Greyrock.

So the children never knew the end of the story ...

Examples

The children and the two pirates were sitting by a ....fire........ .

The .taller pirate. was called Greyrock.

Questions

1 Greyrock told the children a story about a frightening ....
2 Greyrock's .... told him this story a long time ago.
3 In the story, two pirates were .... together quietly.
4 The waves were getting ....
5 .... were swimming round and round the ship.
6 Jack suddenly wanted to .... some food instead!
7 The children and the shorter pirate never heard the .... !

10

G Write words that have the same end sound.

| bear | caught | go | hurry | these | more | eight | shoe |

1 know ....go........
2 knees ....
3 taught ....
4 air ....
5 worry ....
6 sure ....
7 threw ....
8 skate ....

H Complete the words and design weather symbols.

1 w _ _ d
2 r _ _ n
3 f _ g
4 i _ e
5 s _ _ _ m
6 s _ n
7 s _ _ w

I 04 Listen and draw the weather.

11

Accompanying audio tracks can be found on Presentation plus or online

Let's say!

Optional pronunciation practice at the back of the Student's Book focuses on initial key sounds to develop early speaking skills. Supported by accompanying audio.

Let's speak!

Optional extra speaking practice at the back of the Student's Book allows learners to practise the language needed for the Speaking part of the Cambridge English: Flyers test.

How could teachers use *Storyfun 6*?

1 Encourage learners to predict the general topic of the story using flashcards and the story pictures.
2 Teach or revise any Cambridge English: Flyers words that are important in the story.
3 Play the audio or read the story.
4 (Optional) Discuss the story 'value' with learners. You will probably need to do this in your learners' first language to fully explore what the story teaches the reader.
5 Present the vocabulary and general comprehension tasks (usually Activities A–C).
6 Present the grammar, vocabulary and skills sections (generally Activities D–H).
7 Encourage collaborative learning with the *Let's have fun!* pages at the back of the Student's Book.
8 Follow communicative pair- or group-work suggestions in the *Let's speak!* pages at the back of the Student's Book.
9 Use extension activities in the Teacher's Book or set homework tasks.

How is the Teacher's Book organised?

Main topics and grammar
Cambridge English: Flyers topics and grammar focused on in the activities in this unit.

Story summary

Main vocabulary
Cambridge English: Flyers vocabulary focused on in the activities in this unit.

✔ Test tasks for Flyers
Authentic activities that follow the exact format of Cambridge English: Flyers test tasks.

➡ Practice for Flyers
Specific activities that gently build up learners' familiarity and practise for the Cambridge English: Flyers test.

Equipment
Any equipment or materials needed for teaching the unit, including photocopiables, digital flashcards, audio.

Activity notes
A, B, C, etc. sections correspond to Student's Book activities.

🅐 Interactive activity
Activity that can also be completed interactively on Presentation plus.

Answer keys
Answers or suggested answers.

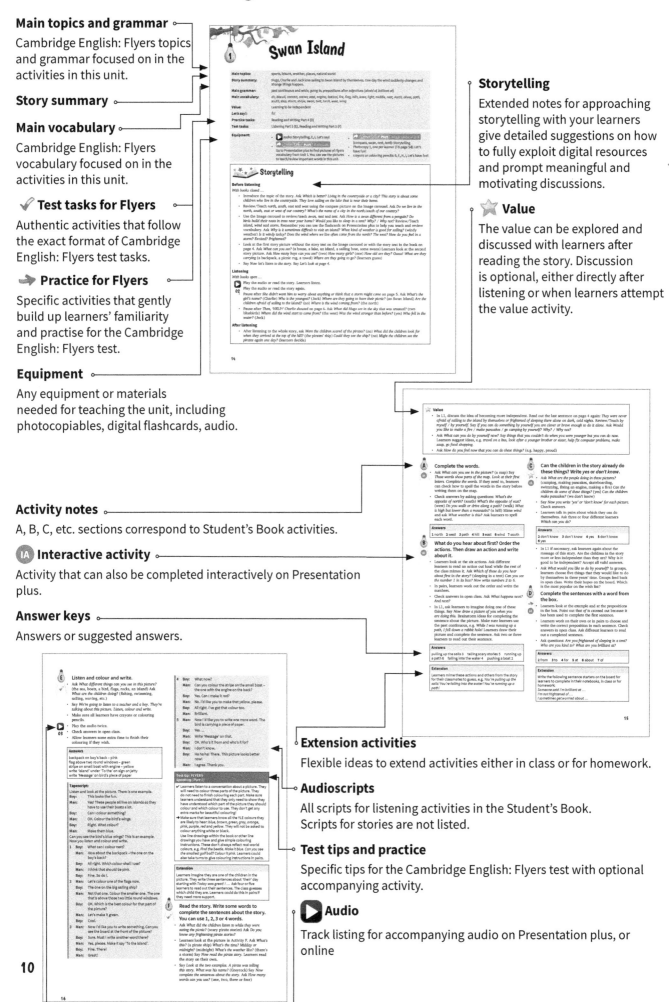

Storytelling
Extended notes for approaching storytelling with your learners give detailed suggestions on how to fully exploit digital resources and prompt meaningful and motivating discussions.

⭐ Value
The value can be explored and discussed with learners after reading the story. Discussion is optional, either directly after listening or when learners attempt the value activity.

Extension activities
Flexible ideas to extend activities either in class or for homework.

Audioscripts
All scripts for listening activities in the Student's Book. Scripts for stories are not listed.

Test tips and practice
Specific tips for the Cambridge English: Flyers test with optional accompanying activity.

▶ Audio
Track listing for accompanying audio on Presentation plus, or online

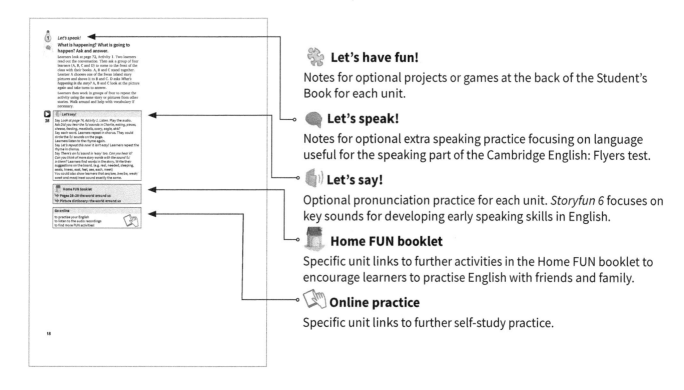

🧩 Let's have fun!

Notes for optional projects or games at the back of the Student's Book for each unit.

💬 Let's speak!

Notes for optional extra speaking practice focusing on language useful for the speaking part of the Cambridge English: Flyers test.

🔊 Let's say!

Optional pronunciation practice for each unit. *Storyfun 6* focuses on key sounds for developing early speaking skills in English.

🏠 Home FUN booklet

Specific unit links to further activities in the Home FUN booklet to encourage learners to practise English with friends and family.

👆 Online practice

Specific unit links to further self-study practice.

How is the digital organised?

Presentation plus

🅐 Interactive activities

Every 'Activity A' in each unit is interactive to check vocabulary comprehension after reading the story and encourage whole-class participation. Other IA activities can be used as a supporting feature, either as a means of introducing an activity, scaffolding, or during answer feedback.

▶ Audio

Audio can be launched from the audio icon. Accompanying audioscripts can be displayed on screen.

Answer key

All activities have a visual answer key to easily display and check answers with your learners.

Digital flashcards

All Cambridge English: Flyers test words are supported with visual flashcards with accompanying audio.

Image carousel

These additional images can be used to prompt further discussion on themes and concepts. Ideas of when and how to use them are within the teacher's notes for each unit.

Each story also has a collection of separate images of the Student's Book pictures without text to prompt discussion before learners open their books and listen, revise the story if heard in a previous lesson or to use as a wrapping-up activity where learners can re-tell the story they've listened to.

Online practice

For the Teacher
o   Presentation plus
o   All audio recordings
o   Additional digital resources to support your classes

For the Student
o   Fun activities to practise the exam, skills and language
o   All audio recordings
o   Additional digital resources to support your classes

Word FUN World app

Checklist for Cambridge English: Flyers

Storyfun 6 provides learners with examples of all Cambridge English: Flyers test tasks.

Paper	Part	Task	Unit
Listening 25 minutes	1	Draw lines between names and people in a picture.	Test: 4
	2	Write words or numbers in a form.	Practice: 4 Test: 5
	3	Match pictures with illustrated words.	Practice: 8 Test: 6
	4	Tick boxes under the correct picture.	Practice: 2, 7 Test: 8
	5	Colour or write in parts of a picture.	Practice: 5 Test: 1
Reading and Writing 40 minutes	1	Copy correct words next to definitions.	Practice: 2, 4, 5, 6, 8 Test: 3
	2	Choose correct responses by circling a letter.	Practice: 6 Test: 2
	3	Choose and copy missing words into a story text.	Practice: 7 Test: 6
	4	Complete a text by copying the correct grammatical words.	Practice: 1, 3, 7, 8 Test: 4
	5	Complete sentences about a story by writing one, two, three or four words.	Practice: 5, 8 Test: 1
	6	Write words in gapped diary/letter. No words are given.	Test: 2, 7
	7	Write a short story by describing events in three pictures.	Practice: 2, 3 Test: 8
Speaking 7–9 minutes	1	Talk about the differences between two pictures.	Practice: 6 Test: 7
	2	Ask and answer questions about people or objects.	Test: 5
	3	Tell a story by describing pictures.	Practice: 2, 8 Test: 3
	4	Answer personal questions.	Practice: 4

Map of the Student's Book

Story and Unit	Value	Topics	Grammar	Test tasks for Flyers
1 Swan Island	Learning to be independent	sports leisure weather places natural world	past continuous and *while* *going to* prepositions after adjectives (*afraid of, brilliant at*)	Reading and Writing Part 5 Listening Part 5
2 Brilliant bikes	Being friendly (*"Hurrah! Well done!"*)	materials transport	*will* *going to* past continuous *ago* *already*	Reading and Writing Parts 2 and 6
3 Frank's funny shopping trip	Listening carefully	animals places in a town	present perfect past continuous + *still*	Reading and Writing Part 1 Speaking Part 3
4 A cake for a queen	Showing kindness (*"This is for you!"*)	food cooking	present perfect *yet* *still* *ago*	Reading and Writing Part 4 Listening Part 1
5 Katy's favourite song	Encouraging your friends and others (*"Don't worry."* *"Come on!"*)	music	*will* *going to* *ask somebody to do something* present perfect	Listening Part 2 Speaking Part 2
6 William's strangest story	Remaining calm	school home materials	*What's it for?* *It's for …*	Reading and Writing Part 3 Listening Part 3
7 The past and the future	Being inspired by people (*"Let me try!"*)	transport IT home	*still* *ago* *will* (prediction) *could* (hypothetical) *should* *by myself/yourself* tenses review	Reading and Writing Part 6 Speaking Part 1
8 The School of Science	Being curious (*"It's so interesting!"*)	school work jobs	*still* *will* *going to* present continuous prepositions of time	Reading and Writing Part 7 Listening Part 4

Swan Island

Main topics:	sports, leisure, weather, places, natural world
Story summary:	Hugo, Charlie and Jack love sailing to Swan Island by themselves. One day the wind suddenly changes and strange things happen.
Main grammar:	past continuous and *while, going to*, prepositions after adjectives (*afraid of, brilliant at*)
Main vocabulary:	*air, biscuit, concert, corner, east, engine, festival, fire, flag, hills, knee, light, middle, nest, north, olives, path, south, step, storm, stripe, swan, tent, torch, west, wing*
Value:	Learning to be independent
Let's say!:	/iː/
Practice tasks:	Reading and Writing Part 4 (D)
Test tasks:	Listening Part 5 (E), Reading and Writing Part 5 (F)

Equipment:	• audio: Storytelling, E, I, Let's say!	• (presentation **PLUS**) Image carousel 1–4 (compass, swan, nest, tent): Storytelling
	• (presentation **PLUS**) flashcards Go to Presentation plus to find pictures of Flyers vocabulary from Unit 1. You can use the pictures to teach/review important words in this unit.	• Photocopy 1, one per learner (TB page 54): Let's have fun! • crayons or colouring pencils: B, E, H, I, Let's have fun!

Storytelling

Before listening

With books closed …

- Introduce the topic of the story. Ask *Which is better? Living in the countryside or a city? This story is about some children who live in the countryside. They love sailing on the lake that is near their home.*
- Review/Teach *north, south, east* and *west* using the compass picture on the Image carousel. Ask *Do we live in the north, south, east or west of our country? What's the name of a city in the north/south of our country?*
- Use the Image carousel to review/teach *swan, nest* and *tent*. Ask *How is a swan different from a penguin? Do birds build their nests in trees near your home? Would you like to sleep in a tent? Why? / Why not?* Review/Teach *island, wind* and *storm*. Remember you can use the flashcards on Presentation plus to help you teach and review vocabulary. Ask *Why is it sometimes difficult to visit an island? What kind of weather is good for sailing?* (windy weather) *Is it windy today? Does the wind where we live often come from the north? The west? How do you feel in a storm? Excited? Frightened?*
- Look at the first story picture without the story text on the Image carousel or with the story text in the book on page 4. Ask *What can you see?* (a house, a lake, an island, a sailing boat, some swans) Learners look at the second story picture. Ask *How many boys can you see?* (two) *How many girls?* (one) *How old are they? Guess! What are they carrying* (a backpack, a picnic rug, a towel) *Where are they going to go?* (learners guess)
- Say *Now let's listen to the story.* Say *Let's look at page 4.*

Listening

With books open …

02

- Play the audio or read the story. Learners listen.
- Play the audio or read the story again.
- Pause after *She didn't want him to worry about anything or think that a storm might come* on page 5. Ask *What's the girl's name?* (Charlie) *Who is the youngest?* (Jack) *Where are they going to have their picnic?* (on Swan Island) *Are the children afraid of sailing to the island?* (no) *Where is the wind coming from?* (the north)
- Pause after *Then, 'HELP!' Charlie shouted* on page 6. Ask *What did Hugo see in the sky that was unusual?* (two bluebirds) *Where did the wind start to come from?* (the west) *Was the wind stronger than before?* (yes) *Who fell in the water?* (Jack)

After listening

- After listening to the whole story, ask *Were the children scared of the pirates?* (no) *What did the children look for when they arrived at the top of the hill?* (the pirates' ship) *Could they see the ship?* (no) *Might the children see the pirates again one day?* (learners decide)

Value

- In L1, discuss the idea of becoming more independent. Read out the last sentence on page 4 again: *They were never afraid of sailing to the island by themselves or frightened of sleeping there alone on dark, cold nights.* Review/Teach *by myself / by yourself.* Say *If you can do something by yourself you are clever or brave enough to do it alone.* Ask *Would you like to make a fire / make pancakes / go camping by yourself? Why? / Why not?*
- Ask *What can you do by yourself now?* Say things that you couldn't do when you were younger but you can do now. Learners suggest ideas, e.g. *travel on a bus, look after a younger brother or sister, help fix computer problems, make soup, go food shopping.*
- Ask *How do you feel now that you can do these things?* (e.g. happy, proud)

A Complete the words.

- Ask *What can you see in the picture?* (a map) Say *These words show parts of the map. Look at their first letters. Complete the words.* If they need to, learners can check how to spell the words in the story before writing them on the map.
- Check answers by asking questions: *What's the opposite of north?* (south) *What's the opposite of east?* (west) *Do you walk or drive along a path?* (walk) *What is high but lower than a mountain?* (a hill) Mime *wind* and ask *What weather is this?* Ask learners to spell each word.

Answers
1 north **2** west **3** path **4** hill **5** east **6** wind **7** south

B What do you hear about first? Order the actions. Then draw an action and write about it.

- Learners look at the six actions. Ask different learners to read an action out loud while the rest of the class mimes it. Ask *Which of these do you hear about first in the story?* (sleeping in a tent) *Can you see the number 1 in its box? Now write numbers 2 to 6.*
- In pairs, learners work out the order and write the numbers.
- Check answers in open class. Ask *What happens next? And next?*
- In L1, ask learners to imagine doing one of these things. Say *Now draw a picture of you when you are doing this.* Brainstorm ideas for completing the sentence about the picture. Make sure learners use the past continuous, e.g. *While I was running up a path, I fell down a rabbit hole!* Learners draw their picture and complete the sentence. Ask two or three learners to read out their sentence.

Answers
pulling up the sails 3   telling scary stories 5   running up a path 6   falling into the water 4   pushing a boat 2

Extension
Learners mime these actions and others from the story for their classmates to guess, e.g. *You're pulling up the sails! You're falling into the water! You're running up a path!*

C Can the children in the story already do these things? Write *yes* or *don't know*.

- Ask *What are the people doing in these pictures?* (camping, making pancakes, skateboarding, swimming, fixing an engine, making a fire) *Can the children do some of these things?* (yes) *Can the children make pancakes?* (we don't know)
- Say *Now you write 'yes' or 'don't know' for each picture.* Check answers.
- Learners talk in pairs about which they can do themselves. Ask three or four different learners *Which can you do?*

Answers
2 don't know   **3** don't know   **4** yes   **5** don't know   **6** yes

- In L1 if necessary, ask learners again about the message of this story. Are the children in the story more or less independent than they are? Why is it good to be independent? Accept all valid answers.
- Ask *What would you like to do by yourself?* In groups, learners choose five things that they would like to do by themselves in three years' time. Groups feed back in open class. Write their hopes on the board. Which is the most popular on the wish list?

D Complete the sentences with a word from the box.

- Learners look at the example and at the prepositions in the box. Point out that *of* is crossed out because it has been used to complete the first sentence.
- Learners work on their own or in pairs to choose and write the correct preposition in each sentence. Check answers in open class. Ask different learners to read out a completed sentence.
- Ask questions: *Are you frightened of sleeping in a tent? Who are you kind to? What are you brilliant at?*

Answers
2 from   **3** to   **4** for   **5** at   **6** about   **7** of

Extension
Write the following sentence starters on the board for learners to complete in their notebooks, in class or for homework: *Someone said I'm brilliant at …* *I'm not frightened of …* *I sometimes get worried about …*

E Listen and colour and write.

- Ask *What different things can you see in this picture?* (the sea, boats, a bird, flags, rocks, an island) Ask *What are the children doing?* (fishing, swimming, sailing, waving, etc.)
- Say *We're going to listen to a teacher and a boy. They're talking about this picture. Listen, colour and write.*
- Make sure all learners have crayons or colouring pencils.

03
- Play the audio twice.
- Check answers in open class.
- Allow learners some extra time to finish their colouring if they wish.

Answers

backpack on boy's back – pink
flag above two round windows – green
stripe on small boat with engine – yellow
write 'island' under 'To the' on sign on jetty
write 'Message' on bird's piece of paper

Tapescript:

Listen and look at the picture. There is one example.

Boy:	This looks like fun.
Man:	Yes! These people all live on islands so they have to use their boats a lot.
Boy:	Can I colour something?
Man:	OK. Colour the bird's wings.
Boy:	Right. What colour?
Man:	Make them blue.

Can you see the bird's blue wings? This is an example. Now you listen and colour and write.

1	Boy:	What can I colour next?
	Man:	How about the backpack – the one on the boy's back?
	Boy:	All right. Which colour shall I use?
	Man:	I think that should be pink.
	Boy:	Fine. So do I.
2	Man:	Let's colour one of the flags now.
	Boy:	The one on the big sailing ship?
	Man:	Not that one. Colour the smaller one. The one that's above those two little round windows.
	Boy:	OK. Which is the best colour for that part of the picture?
	Man:	Let's make it green.
	Boy:	Cool.
3	Man:	Now I'd like you to write something. Can you see the board at the front of the picture?
	Boy:	Sure. Must I write another word there?
	Man:	Yes, please. Make it say 'To the island'.
	Boy:	Fine. There!
	Man:	Great!

4	Boy:	What now?
	Man:	Can you colour the stripe on the small boat – the one with the engine on the back?
	Boy:	Yes. Can I make it red?
	Man:	No. I'd like you to make that yellow, please.
	Boy:	All right. I've got that colour too.
	Man:	Brilliant.
5	Man:	Now I'd like you to write one more word. The bird is carrying a piece of paper.
	Boy:	Yes …
	Man:	Write 'Message' on that.
	Boy:	OK. Who's it from and who's it for?
	Man:	I don't know.
	Boy:	Ha ha ha! There. This picture looks better now!
	Man:	I agree. Thank you.

Test tip: FLYERS
Speaking (Part 1)

✔ Learners listen to a conversation about a picture. They will need to colour three parts of the picture. They do not need to finish colouring each part. Make sure learners understand that they only need to show they have understood which part of the picture they should colour and which colour to use. They don't get any extra marks for beautiful colouring!

➜ Make sure that learners know all the YLE colours they are likely to hear: *blue, brown, green, grey, orange, pink, purple, red* and *yellow*. They will not be asked to colour anything white or black.

Use line drawings within the book or other line drawings you have and give simple colouring instructions. These don't always reflect real-world colours, e.g. *Find the beetle. Make it blue. Can you see the smallest golf ball? Colour it pink.* Learners could also take turns to give colouring instructions in pairs.

Extension

Learners imagine they are one of the children in the picture. They write three sentences about 'their' day starting with *Today was great! I …* Ask four or five learners to read out their sentences. The class guesses which child they are. Learners could do this in pairs if they need more support.

F Read the story. Write some words to complete the sentences about the story. You can use 1, 2, 3 or 4 words.

- Ask *What did the children listen to while they were eating the picnic?* (scary pirate stories) Ask *Do you know any frightening pirate stories?*
- Learners look at the picture in Activity F. Ask *What's this?* (a pirate ship) *What's the time? Midday or midnight?* (midnight) *What's the weather like?* (there's a storm) Say *Now read the pirate story.* Learners read the story on their own.
- Say *Look at the two examples. A pirate was telling this story. What was his name?* (Greyrock) Say *Now complete the sentences about the story.* Ask *How many words can you use?* (one, two, three or four)

- Learners complete sentences 1–7 on their own as a test task or in pairs. Walk around and help if necessary. Check answers in open class.
- Ask *What happens at the end of the story?* Learners guess.

Test tip: FLYERS
Reading and Writing, Listening (all parts)

Encourage learners to answer all of the tasks, even if their answers are guesses – they may be the right ones!

G Write words that have the same end sound.

- Learners look at the example. Say *Listen. Can you hear the same sound at the end of 'know' and 'go'?* Prompt learners to say /əʊ/ in chorus. Ask *What other words do you know with this sound?* (e.g. oh!, no, slow, throw, alone, most, only, boat)
- Remind learners that *know* and *no* (and *hole/whole* and *road/rode*) sound exactly the same.
- Say *Now find words in the box that have the same end sounds as the words in 2 to 8.* Encourage learners in pairs to say all the words aloud. Check answers.
- Ask *Can you think of any more words with the same end sounds as the words in 2 to 8?* (e.g. 2 bees, 3 bought, 4 hair, 5 curry, 6 door, 7 who, 8 classmate)

Answers

2 these   **3** caught   **4** bear   **5** hurry   **6** more
7 shoe   **8** eight

H Complete the words and design weather symbols.

- Ask *Which weather words do you know?* Do a class brainstorm and write the words on the board. Ask *What kind of weather do you like?* Write on the board: *I like it when it _____ because I can _____ .* Learners talk in pairs to complete the sentence. Ask two or three pairs for their answers.
- Learners look at Activity H. Say *Write the missing letters in the weather words.* Learners complete the words and compare their spellings with a partner. Check answers in open class.
- Say *Now draw a little picture above each weather word.* Explain in L1 that these should be symbols and simple and clear enough to draw quickly in the next activity.

Answers

1 wind   **2** rain   **3** fog   **4** ice   **5** storm   **6** sun   **7** snow

I Listen and draw the weather.

- Point to the map and ask *What's this?* (a map) *What's on the map?* (a forest, a beach, a river, some fields, a town, a castle, an island, some hills)
- Say *Listen to a man on the radio. He's talking about the weather in this part of the country. Listen and draw the weather in the right places.*

- Play the audio.
- Play the audio a second time if necessary and allow time for learners to complete their symbols before checking answers in open class.
- Ask *Can you remember? Which place is good for people who want to go for a walk / fly a kite today?* (Spring Forest / between Greyrock Castle and the beach) *What should you take with you if you go to the village today?* (an umbrella) *Drivers! Is there any ice on the roads today?* (no)

Answers

Spring Forest – sun
South of river / fields – fog
North of hills – storm
Between Greyrock Castle and beach – wind
Village – rain

Tapescript:

And it's good morning from me to everyone today. Here's your weather news. The temperature will be quite low everywhere today, but let's start with Spring Forest. It'll be really sunny there for most of the day, so put your coats on and go for a lovely long walk there if you don't have to work today!
South of the river, it's going to be cold and foggy all day, I'm afraid. There won't be any sun today there for the vegetables in the fields …
And the weather won't be wonderful north of the hills. Dark grey clouds and then a bad storm. Sorry about that. Stay inside!
Between Greyrock Castle (we think a famous pirate lived there a long time ago) and the beach, it's going to be quite windy. That's good news for children who enjoy flying kites. It'll be a great day for doing that.
And the weather in the village? Well, no ice on the roads, but lots of rain today, so don't forget to take umbrellas with you when you go shopping.
And now for some of your favourite pop music …

Extension

Learners pretend to be presenters on TV. They use this map (or invent another one) and their symbols to help them present their own weather forecast. They can prepare and practise the forecast in pairs and take turns to talk about different places on the map. Ask two or three pairs to present their forecast to the rest of the class.

Let's have fun!

Choose your own answers to questions about a story called 'The Young Pirate'. Then design the front cover of your book.

Learners look at page 68, Activity 1. Say *Look at the book. What's it about?* (a pirate) Learners read the questions and in pairs choose their answers. Then give each learner Photocopy 1 (TB page 54). They design their book cover and then complete the text about the book using full-sentence answers to the questions. Learners could take turns to show their design to the class and read out their description of the story.

Let's speak!

What is happening? What is going to happen? Ask and answer.

Learners look at page 72, Activity 1. Two learners read out the conversation. Then ask a group of four learners (A, B, C and D) to come to the front of the class with their books. A, B and C stand together. Learner A chooses one of the Swan Island story pictures and shows it to B and C. D asks *What's happening in the story?* A, B and C look at the picture again and take turns to answer.

Learners then work in groups of four to repeat the activity using the same story or pictures from other stories. Walk around and help with vocabulary if necessary.

▶
28

 Let's say!

Say *Look at page 74, Activity 1. Listen.* Play the audio.
Ask *Did you hear the /iː/ sounds in Charlie, eating, pieces, cheese, feeding, meatballs, scary, eagle, skis?*
Say each word. Learners repeat in chorus. They could circle the /iː/ sounds on the page.
Learners listen to the rhyme again.
Say *Let's repeat this now! It isn't easy!* Learners repeat the rhyme in chorus.
Say *There's an /iː/ sound in 'easy' too. Can you hear it? Can you think of more story words with the sound /iː/ in them?* Learners find words in the story. Write their suggestions on the board. (e.g. real, needed, sleeping, seats, knees, east, feel, see, each, meet)
You could also show learners that *sea/see, bee/be, weak/ week* and *meat/meet* sound exactly the same.

Home FUN booklet

➡ Pages 28–29 the world around us
➡ Picture dictionary: the world around us

Go online

to practise your English
to listen to the audio recordings
to find more FUN activities!

Brilliant bikes

2

Main topics:	materials, transport
Story summary:	Holly builds a new bike for the race. Her unfriendly neighbour Victoria has a new bike. Holly helps Victoria when she has a problem.
Main grammar:	*will, going to,* past continuous, *ago, already*
Main vocabulary:	*amazing, cycle, design, engine, expensive, fast, glue, invent, metal, piece, plastic, racing, silver, tyre, wheel, wonderful, wood*
Value:	Being friendly (*"Hurrah! Well done!"*)
Let's say!:	/ɔː/
Practice tasks:	Reading and Writing Part 1 (A), Listening Part 4 (E), Reading and Writing Part 7 (G), Speaking Part 3 (G)
Test tasks:	Reading and Writing Part 2 (F), Reading and Writing Part 6 (I)
Equipment:	• audio: Storytelling, E, H, Let's say! • **presentation PLUS** flashcards Go to Presentation plus to find pictures of Flyers vocabulary from Unit 2. You can use the pictures to teach/review important words in this unit.	• **presentation PLUS** Image carousel 5–7 (bicycle, garage, spanner): Storytelling • Photocopy 2, one per group of learners (TB page 55): Storytelling Extension • paper, scissors: Storytelling Extension • paper: Let's have fun!

 Storytelling

Before listening

With books closed …

- Introduce the topic of the story. Ask about bikes: *Do you have a bike? Do you like riding your bike? Where do you ride your bike? To school? If you don't have a bike, would you like one?* Say *This story is about a girl who loves making things. In this story she builds a bike.*
- Use the Image carousel picture to review/teach *bicycle* and *to cycle.* Mime *cycling* and underline *cycle* in *bicycle* to show the link between the words. Ask *Do you cycle to (the sports centre)? Is cycling fun or boring?* Use the Image carousel picture of the bicycle to also review/teach *tyre.*
- Say *When a part of your bicycle breaks, you have to fix it. Who fixes a car when a car breaks?* (a mechanic) Use the Image carousel pictures to teach *garage* and *spanner.*
- Mime *wobble.* Say *Little children wobble when they first learn to ride a bike!*
- Remember you can use the flashcards on Presentation plus to help you teach and review vocabulary.
- Look at the first story picture without the story text on the Image carousel or with the story text in the book on page 12. Ask *What's this story about?* (learners guess) *What is the girl with dark hair doing?* (riding a bike / cycling) *Another girl is looking at a …* (poster) *How old are these two girls? Guess!*
- Say *Now let's listen to the story.* Say *Let's look at page 12.*

Listening

With books open …

▶ Play the audio or read the story. Learners listen.

05 Play the audio or read the story again.

- Pause after *She ran upstairs and knocked on the door* on page 13. Ask *What is the name of the girl in the story?* (Holly) *What did she read about in town?* (a bike race) *What did she decide to do?* (make a new bike) *She needs a new bike because her old one is too …* (small/slow) *What is going to happen next?* (learners guess)
- Pause after *They started to work and they worked all day until the bike was ready* on page 14. Ask *Who helped Holly to build her bike?* (her grandfather / Grandpa) *Which two things did Holly's grandfather give her?* (the tyre, the spanner) *Is Victoria a kind girl?* (learners decide) *Who might win the race?* (learners guess)

After listening

- After listening to the whole story, ask *Who was the winner?* (both girls) *Would you like to enter a race like this? Why? / Why not? Would you like to change the end of this story? How? Have you got something that is very special, like Holly's spanner?* Learners answer.

Value

- In L1, discuss the idea of making friends and the importance of trying to be kind to others. Ask *How is Holly kind?* (Victoria wasn't nice to her, but Holly helps Victoria when she has a problem with her bike.) *What does Holly say when she helps Victoria?* (Don't worry! I can help you.) Discuss with learners why sometimes people find it hard to be kind. Do this sensitively.
- Ask *Is it important to make friends? Why? How can you make friends? How do good friends help each other?* Learners could discuss this in small groups or in open class.

Extension

Sit small groups of learners round different tables. Give each group a sheet of paper to write eight words on and Photocopy 2 (TB page 55) and pairs of scissors. Learners cut the page up so each letter is in a separate square. Groups put all the letters face up on their table.

Say *I'm going to say eight different words. Listen carefully. Fix, enough, forty, tomorrow, because, story, Grandpa, bicycle.*

Pause between each word to give learners time to write it down. Each group writes the eight words on a piece of paper. They check their spellings. (All these words are in this unit.)

Say *Go!* Learners work together as quickly as possible to make each word with their letters, placing them in rows on their table.

The group that finishes first shouts *We've finished!* Allow the other groups time to finish.

If words are spelled correctly, six letters will be left: *eedhnt.* Ask *Which two words can you spell with these letters?* (the end)

A   Draw lines. Make sentences

- Learners look at the example and read the other five sentence starters on their own. They draw lines to match them to the correct endings. They check their answers in pairs. Different pairs read out one of the completed sentences in open class.
- Ask different learners *Do you practise something? How often do you practise that?*

Answers

2 design things like cars.   **3** you get better at something.   **4** you go as fast as you can.   **5** is a great sport.   **6** makes a motorbike move.

B   Put the sentences in order. Write numbers.

- Learners read the seven sentences A–G on their own and look at the number *1* next to sentence D. Say *This was the first thing here that happened in the story.* Ask *What happened next?* (learners suggest an answer)
- In pairs, learners write numbers *2–7* in the appropriate boxes.
- Check answers in open class. Ask one learner to read out sentence 2. Ask the class if they agree or disagree. Continue with the other answers in the same way, in the order they appear in the story.

Answers

A 5   **B** 2   **C** 4   (**D** 1)   **E** 7   **F** 3   **G** 6

Extension

For homework or in class, learners write a summary of the story in their notebooks, copying the sentences from Activity B. They can add other interesting information about the story if they like.

C   Who did this? Write A (Holly), B (Grandpa) or C (Victoria).

- Learners look at picture 1. Ask *What's this person doing?* (playing the piano) *Who plays the piano in the story?* (Victoria) *Which letter shows that Victoria did this?* (C) Ask *Who did these other things?*
- In pairs or on their own, learners look at pictures 2–6 and write *A*, *B* or *C* in the boxes. If they need help, learners can find the answers in the story.

Answers

2 B   **3** A   **4** B   **5** A   **6** C

D   Which is David's friendliest answer (A, B or C)? Write friendly answers for the other sentences.

- In L1 if necessary, ask learners again about the message of this story. Ask two or three different learners *What kind things do you do for your friends and the people in your family?*
- Learners look at Activity D. They read the example and the three answer options. Ask *Which is the kindest answer?* (B) *Why aren't A and C kind answers?* Discuss this in L1. (A sounds as though they don't want to accept the apology so they say they are in a hurry. C doesn't accept the apology, but perhaps they have a reason for speaking like that.)
- Learners then look at the four other speech bubbles. Say *Write kind answers.* Learners work in pairs to complete the responses. Write their suggestions on the board.

Suggested answers

Oh dear. Don't worry.
Do you? Fantastic!
I can help if you want.
I've got a map. Let's find out.

Extension

Learners use some of these sentences to write and then perform a mini role play about being kind and making friends. For example:

A: *My front wheel is broken.*
B: *Oh dear. Don't worry. I can help you. I've got a spanner.*
A: *Can you fix it?*
B: *Yes. It works now.*
A: *Thank you! That's fantastic!*

E · Listen and tick the box.

- Learners read the poster again on page 12. Ask *Who can tell Holly more about the race?* (Richard Black) *How can Holly ask Richard questions about the race? She can send him an ...* (email) *or she can ...* (phone him)
- Learners work in small groups to decide which questions to ask Richard about the race. Give them plenty of time to do this. Write five or six of their suggestions on the board and leave them there, e.g.

  How many people will there be in the race?

  Where does the race start/finish?

  What time does the race start/finish?

  Will the race be difficult?

  What kind of clothes should people wear?

- Tell learners they are going to hear Holly and Richard talking on the phone. Learners look at the first question in Activity E and the first set of pictures. Ask *What must you do?* (tick A, B or C) Before they listen, learners could guess which answers are right.
- Play the audio. Learners listen and tick the answers. Play the audio again. Learners check their own answers. Then check answers in open class.
- Ask *Should we always wear cycle helmets? If you ride a bike and have a helmet, what colour is yours?*

06

Answers
1 C **2** B **3** A

Tapescript:

1 What time does the race start?

  Girl: Hello, Richard. What time does the bike race start?

  Man: It begins at eleven fifteen, Holly. But you must be ready to start before that.

  Girl: OK. I'll be there at ten thirty then.

  Man: Great! Will your parents come and watch?

  Girl: Sure! I'll ask them to stand next to the starting line at a quarter to eleven.

2 Which number must Holly wear on her T-shirt?

  Girl: I think I have to wear the number 23 on my T-shirt. Is that right?

  Man: I've got the information here, Holly. Let me see ... No ...

  Girl: Is it 43 then? I can't remember.

  Man: Oh! Here it is! Your number's 32.

  Girl: Great! Thanks.

3 Who gave Holly a helmet?

  Man: Don't forget, Holly. You must wear a helmet in the race. It's dangerous to ride without one.

  Girl: Oh, I know, Richard. I've already got one.

  Man: Excellent. Did your uncle buy that for you?

  Girl: No. A classmate gave it to me, actually.

  Man: Oh!

  Girl: My grandma's just bought one too. She also loves cycling!

Extension

Look at the questions to ask Richard on the board again. Ask *Which of these questions did Holly ask Richard?* Erase those questions. In pairs, learners choose answers to the remaining questions. Then they role play the questions and answers conversation. Walk round and help with vocabulary if necessary. Focus on fluency rather than accuracy at this point.

F · Holly is talking to her uncle. What does Holly say? Choose the best answer. Write a letter (A–H).

- Say *To build her bike, Holly needed some things that were made of metal and plastic. Who did she ask for these?* (her mum and her uncle)
- Learners look at the picture of Holly's uncle. Ask *What's he doing?* (he's fixing his motorbike)
- Learners look at the example. Ask two learners to read out the question and the answer marked *A*. Say *Holly's uncle asked a question. Holly answered it.* Learners could cross out *A* from Holly's possible answers.
- Say *Now you match the answers to the questions. Write the letter. There are two answers in A to H you don't need.* Learners complete this on their own as a test task or work in pairs, reading the conversation and choosing one of Holly's answers for each gap.
- Check answers in open class, asking pairs to read out each exchange in full.
- Ask *Is building a bike easy or difficult? What kind of person is Holly? She's ...* (clever/brave/excited) *What can you build?*

Answers
1 E **2** H **3** F **4** B **5** D

Test tip: FLYERS
Reading and Writing (Part 2)

✔ Learners have to fill in one person's part of a two-way conversation. Learners have to choose five answers from seven (excluding the example). Given sentences are often questions. Only one answer will be correct for each turn and it should not only fit the context but also be grammatically correct. Learners should read the whole text before they start to choose and fill in the missing sentences.

→ Give learners practice in creating mini-conversations by completing missing lines, e.g. groups decide what B is saying here:

A: *I took lots of photos at the concert. Did you?*
B: ...
A: *How often do you listen to music online?*
B: ...

G · Look, talk and choose answers. Then write about the picture.

- Learners look at the picture. Ask *Where is Holly?* (in her garden / outside the garage) *What is she holding?* (a wheel) *What else can you see?* (a swing, two trees, an umbrella, four parrots, a building, some flowers)

What is the weather like? (it's sunny)

- Explain, in L1 if necessary, that you can see the answers to some of the questions but have to imagine the answers to others. Learners choose their answers in pairs.

- Say *Now write about the picture.* When they have finished, ask different learners to read out their answers in open class.

> **Suggested answer**
>
> Holly is in the garden now. Her flat is on the first floor. Holly is holding a wheel. She is thinking about the race. Four parrots are in the sky. They think Holly is going to feed them.

Listen and draw a line from the start to the end of the race.

- Ask *Where did Holly cycle?* (around the lake, through the wood, over the hills and the river and past the farms) Learners read the route part of the story again on page 14.

- Review/Teach *around, past, over* and *through.* Model these in the classroom. Walk around a table where learners are sitting. Draw a circle in the air as you say *I'm walking **around** you.* Walk past a table and wave to learners who are sitting at it. Say *Hello. Now I'm walking **past** you. Goodbye!* Using your fingers, mime someone's legs jumping over a book. Say *My fingers are jumping **over** this book.* Put your arm through an open-ended box and say *I'm putting my arm **through** this box.*

- Say *Look at the map. Find the start.* (learners point) *Find the finish.* (learners point) *What else can you see on the map?* Say *You are going to hear Holly's grandfather telling you where Holly cycled.*

07

- Play the audio. Learners listen and draw a line (in pencil) to show where Holly cycled. Learners compare their answers. Play the audio a second time if necessary.

- Learners show each other their maps. Ask *Which farm did Holly not cycle past?* (Sheepstay Farm) Walk around and check that learners have drawn their lines correctly.

> **Tapescript:**
>
> It was a brilliant race! Holly began at the starting line with all the others. That was at the top of Toowomba Lake. Lots of the parents were there and many clapped and shouted, 'You can do it! Good luck, everyone!' We were there too!
>
> The children rode around the lake. Then they went along the road that goes to Grey Wood. Grey Wood is full of interesting animals. You'll always see big lizards there. Sometimes blue lizards. They love to lie in the sun on the rocks between the trees.
>
> After the children cycled through the wood, they rode along the road that goes between the two lower hills and then cycled to the top of Cloud Hill. That's the highest hill near here. You can see a long way from up there. Then they cycled down the hill ('That was fun,' Holly said) and over the bridge – the one that crosses Crocodile River. I've never seen any crocodiles there, but someone else did once.

> Then the children cycled past Duck Farm. After that, they turned right and then turned left at Kangaroo Fields. After Kangaroo Fields, they turned right again. From there, they could see some of the taller city buildings. We waited for Holly at the finishing line in the city.
>
> We were so pleased when she and Victoria won. I think they will be good friends now.

> **Extension**
>
> Say *Imagine you are one of the parrots in the picture on page 18. You are hiding somewhere in the map. Can your friend guess where you are?* Learners take turns to ask yes/no questions to find the parrot, e.g. *Are you in May Lake? Are you behind Cloud Hill? Are you next to Sheepstay Farm?*

Read Holly's message and write the missing words. Write one word on each line.

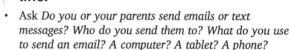

- Ask *Do you or your parents send emails or text messages? Who do you send them to? What do you use to send an email? A computer? A tablet? A phone?*

- Say *Look at Holly's email. Who did she send this to?* (George) *When did she send it?* (on 18 June)

- Say *Now read the rest of the email. Don't write anything yet.* Ask *Who talked to Holly at the end of the race?* (a journalist) *What will Holly show George tomorrow?* (the spanner)

- Look at the example. Ask *Why is the answer 'was' and not 'is'?* (Holly wrote the message after the race.)

- Say *Now write one word in each gap.* Learners read the message again and complete the gaps on their own as a test task or work with a partner to see if they chose the same answers.

> **Answers**
>
> **1** the **2** drink/glass/bottle/cup **3** asked **4** them **5** to

> **Test tip: FLYERS**
> *Reading and Writing (Part 6)*
>
> ✔ Learners need to complete a diary entry, a message or a letter. There are five one-word gaps and the example. The missing words are always from the Starters, Movers or Flyers word lists. Some gaps will be grammatical, e.g. *this, it, a, or, mine, because, since.* Other gaps will be lexical, e.g. *bought, reading, photo, café, walk, water.*
>
> → Using any interesting text, you might blank out a mixture of grammatical and lexical words for learners to guess. Accept any reasonable answers.

Let's have fun!

Think about safety on your bike. Make a poster.

Learners look at page 68, Activity 2 and brainstorm their ideas in pairs. Ask learners to talk about their ideas for keeping safe in open class.

Give each learner a piece of paper. Learners work on their own or in pairs to complete their bike safety posters. If possible, display the posters on the classroom wall.

2 Let's speak!

Ask and answer about your week.

Learners look at page 72, Activity 2. Ask different learners *What are you going to do tomorrow? What are you going to do after school on Thursday?* Encourage learners to use *I may …* and *I might …* in their replies if they are not sure. Generate lots of ideas for activities learners might do. Learners then take turns to ask and answer the question in closed pairs. Walk around and help with vocabulary if necessary.

 Let's say!

29

Say *Look at page 74, Activity 2. Listen.* Play the audio.
Ask *Did you hear the /ɔː/ sounds in Victoria, bored, called, bought, four, small, water, walk, saw, dinosaur?*
Say each word. Learners repeat in chorus. They could circle the /ɔː/sounds on the page.
Learners listen to the rhyme again.
Say *Let's all say this together now!* Learners repeat the rhyme in chorus.
Say *There's an /ɔː/ sound in 'all' too. Can you hear it? Can you think of more story words with the sound /ɔː/ in them?* Learners find words in the story. Write their suggestions on the board. (e.g. wall, thought, your, floor, door, morning, forty, always, already)
You could also show learners that *bored/board* and *for/four* sound exactly the same.

Home FUN booklet

➡ **Pages 14–15 and 24–25 materials, transport**
➡ **Picture dictionary: transport**

Go online

to practise your English
to listen to the audio recordings
to find more FUN activities!

3 Frank's funny shopping trip

Main topics:	animals, places in a town
Story summary:	Frank has a new Amazing Creatures app on his phone. His mum asks him to collect three things for her in town, but he isn't listening carefully.
Main grammar:	present perfect, past continuous + *still*
Main vocabulary:	*bandage, bracelet, butterfly, camel, chemist's, eagle, glass, insect, necklace, nest, octopus, police station, post office, railway station, shampoo, shelf, shoe factory, soap*
Value:	Listening carefully
Let's say!:	/uː/
Practice tasks:	Reading and Writing Part 7 (G), Reading and Writing Part 4 (H)
Test tasks:	Reading and Writing Part 1 (E), Speaking Part 3 (G)

Equipment:	
	• ▶ audio: Storytelling, C, G, Let's say!
	• presentation **PLUS** flashcards
	Go to Presentation plus to find pictures of Flyers vocabulary from Unit 3. You can use the pictures to teach/review important words in this unit.
	• (presentation **PLUS**) Image carousel 8–14 (bracelet, necklace, bandage, shampoo; cushion, shelf, comb): Storytelling, E
	• Photocopy 3, one per learner (TB page 56): Let's have fun!
	• crayons or colouring pencils: Let's have fun!

Storytelling

Before listening

With books closed …

- Introduce the topic of the story. Say *This story is about a boy who goes shopping in town, but he is more interested in looking at his new app! It's about interesting animals.*
- Review/Teach places in town, accepting other valid answers: *Where must you go to catch a train?* (to a railway station) *Where do people often buy stamps?* (at a post office) *Where can you buy medicine and toothpaste?* (at a chemist's) *Where do police officers work at their desks?* (at a police station) *What do we call a place where people use machines to make things like cars or shoes?* (a factory)
- Use the Image carousel to review/teach *bracelet, necklace, bandage* and *shampoo.* Ask *What are sometimes made of gold or silver?* (bracelets/necklaces) *What can you put on a knee or elbow if you hurt it?* (a bandage) *What can we use to wash our hair?* (shampoo)
- Remember you can use the flashcards on Presentation plus to help you teach and review vocabulary.
- Look at the first and second story pictures without the story text on the Image carousel or with the story text in the book on page 20. Say *This is Frank. He is standing on a balcony. Who is he with?* (learners guess – his mum) *What are they talking about?* (learners guess)
- Say *Now let's listen to the story.* Say *Let's look at page 20.*

Listening

With books open …

08

- Play the audio or read the story. Learners listen.
- Play the audio or read the story again.
- Pause after *'No problem!' Frank said and, with his phone in his hand and Mum's money in his pocket, he left the apartment* on page 20. Ask *How many things must Frank collect in town?* (three) *Was Frank listening carefully to his mum?* (no) *What was he looking at?* (his app) *Frank must buy a train ticket. Where to?* (Ingsterness) Ask *Do you think Frank will remember everything?* (learners guess)
- Pause after *'Thanks! Silly me!' Frank said* on page 22. Ask *What did Frank ask for at the train station?* (the cheapest ticket to insects' nests) *What did Frank ask for in the shop between the shoe factory and the post office?* (an old phone) *Frank made mistakes. What was he thinking about?* (butterflies, insects, eagles) *Which friends does Frank see?* (David, Michael, Sophia)

After listening

- After listening to the whole story, ask *What does Frank tell his mum that he got?* (the deepest biscuit from an insects' nest, an old phone, a new gym shoe) *What did he really get?* (the cheapest ticket to Ingsterness, the gold stone for her bracelet, some new shampoo) *What did Frank's mum want him to show her?* (the Amazing Creatures app)

A — Read and write a place from the story.

• Learners look at the words in the five boxes and at the example. Review/Teach *platform* and *timetable*. Ask *Where might you see platforms, a timetable and trains? At …* (a railway station)

• Learners work on their own or in pairs to complete the rest of the task. They can check their spellings by finding the places in the story.

Answers

2 a factory   **3** a chemist's   **4** a post office
5 a police station

Extension

Learners mime being in places from the story, and other places in town, for the class to guess, e.g. *a supermarket, a library, a college, a cinema, a bank, a fire station, an airport, an office, a museum, a theatre, a stadium, a hotel, a restaurant.*

B — Draw lines. Make sentences.

• Learners look at the sentence starters and their endings. Read out the example: *Frank's mum needed three things from …* (the town.) Ask *Can you see the line? Now you draw lines to complete the sentences.*

• Learners work on their own. They could try to complete the activity from memory and then check their answers in the story. Ask different learners to read out a completed sentence in open class.

Answers

2 about eagles.   **3** in a rocket.   **4** of a bracelet.
5 his home.   **6** a basement.   **7** to a post office.

C — Who's talking about the story? Listen and write a name.

• Say *We are going to listen to three children. They are talking about stories they have read. Only one of them has read 'Frank's funny shopping trip'. Listen carefully and write their name.*

 • Play the audio.

09 • Play the audio again. Ask *How do you know that the answer wasn't Emma?* (Frank didn't go home with all the wrong things) *Why wasn't it Pat?* (Frank didn't do the shopping on the internet)

Tapescript:

Emma: Hi, I'm Emma. I've got lots of funny apps on my phone and I loved this story. I like learning interesting things too. But I was surprised that the boy didn't use his phone to call his mother, and then he went home with all the wrong things. Why didn't he think more carefully?

Pat: I'm Pat. My brother and I are both like the boy in the story. We've got apps on our phone as well. Most of them are funny games, but I have got one or two really good ones that help me learn. It was a good idea for Frank to do the shopping on the internet. That's often the easiest way.

Julia: Hello. I'm Julia. I like learning new things too. Apps are great! You can find out all kinds of interesting things. It's nice that the boy in the story shows the information to his friends and I was pleased when he thought carefully about the places he went to. That helped him to remember the shopping!

Answer

Julia

• In L1 if necessary, ask learners again about the message of this story. Say *Frank didn't listen very carefully to his mother when she asked him to do different things. Was it hard or easy for him to remember?* (learners guess) *What does Frank say he should do next time?* (write a list on his phone) *Is that a good idea? Have you got a better idea?* (learners answer)

D — Read about tortoises. Then write about an animal.

• Ask *Which animals do you read about in the story?* (butterflies, eagles, tortoises) *What is your favourite animal? What do you know about it?* (learners talk about their favourite animals)

• Learners look at Activity D. Say *Let's read about tortoises!* Ask three learners to read out one sentence each. Ask *Do tortoises have teeth?* (no) *How long can they live?* (100 years) *When do they sleep?* (in the winter)

• Say *Now you choose an animal to write about. What do you want to know about that animal? Write three questions in your notebook.*

• Learners find answers to their animal questions on the internet or in books. They write a text about their animal, e.g. *Brown bears have strong legs, but they aren't good at climbing trees. Brown bears can live for 20 years. Many brown bears sleep in the winter.*

Extension

In pairs, learners could prepare a short talk about their animal for the class to listen to. If possible, they could do an electronic slide show presentation or use photographs of their animal to help them.

E Look and read. Choose the correct words and write them on the lines.

- Use the Image carousel to review/teach *cushion, shelf* and *comb*.

- Say *The words that are outside the sentences are the possible answers.* Learners complete this as a test task on their own. Alternatively, learners do the task in groups as follows.

- Say *Let's have a race!* Divide the class into small groups. Each group chooses one learner to write. Say *Look at the answers outside the box again. Find and write as quickly as you can the five animal words, four things that you find inside a house or big shop, and six places in town. Go!* Learners write the answers in their notebooks. The first group to finish are the winners. Check answers. (a beetle, an insect, an eagle, a butterfly, a dinosaur; a cushion, a shelf, a comb, an elevator; an airport, a fire station, an office, a bank, a museum, a castle)

- Learners read the example in Activity E. Say *Now you write the answers for 1 to 10.* Learners work in their groups to complete the task, and feed back in open class.

- Ask *Which four words didn't you use?* (a cushion, a beetle, an eagle, an office)

Answers

1 a bank   2 a shelf   3 an elevator   4 a butterfly
5 a castle   6 a dinosaur   7 a comb   8 an airport
9 an insect   10 a museum

Test tip: FLYERS
Reading and Writing (Part 1)

- ✔ There are 15 nouns (singular/plural/uncountable forms) around the ten (plus one example) definitions. Make sure learners understand that four of the nouns will not be correct answers. Learners must copy the answers in the same form and not forget to add the article if necessary, e.g. *swans, an astronaut.*

- ➜ When practising this task, tell learners to check they have copied each of their answers correctly and ask, e.g. *How many letters are there in 'octopus'?* In any lesson, write key or interesting words on the board and tell learners to copy them into interesting topic fact files.

Extension

Learners use the definitions in the task to help them write their own definitions for the four unused answers. They can write one or two sentences for each one.
Suggestions:
This is soft and some people put them on sofas or chairs.
This is a small insect. It often lives under the ground.
This large bird has strong wings. It builds its nest in high places.
This is a room where people often work on computers.

F *I've done* or *I was still doing?* Write the correct form of the verb.

- You may want to review/teach the difference between present perfect and past continuous more fully before learners do this task.

- Write on the board: *Frank <u>was still looking</u> at his app when his mum finished talking to him.* Ask *What was Frank doing when his mum was talking?* (looking at his app) *When his mum stopped talking, what was Frank doing?* (looking at his app!) Say *That's right! Frank didn't stop looking at his app. He was <u>still</u> looking at it while <u>and after</u> his mum talked to him.*

- Explain, in L1 if necessary, that learners need to decide whether the actions here are finished or were continuing. Look at the example together and ask *Has this person finished their homework?* (yes) Say *So we can't say here 'I was still doing all my homework.'* (no)

- Learners complete sentences 3–8 with the verb in the correct form. Walk around and help further if necessary. Check answers in open class.

Answers

3 've found   4 've made   5 was still texting
6 've bought   7 've fixed   8 was still learning

G Look at the pictures and listen. Then tell the story.

- Learners look at the cartoon story. Ask *Are these the same people as in Frank's shopping story?* (no – it's a girl and her grandfather) Say *You are going to help tell this story, but someone is going to start it for you.*

10

- Play the audio. Learners listen to the beginning of the story. Then they practise this as a test task, on their own or in pairs, or as follows.

- Ask *What is the girl's name?* (Emma) *What does she do next?* (go shopping for her grandpa) In open class, ask questions about each picture to prompt full-sentence answers to tell the story.

  Picture 2: Where is Emma now?

  Picture 3: Where is Emma now? What is she doing?

  Picture 4: Where is Emma now? Can she go up in the elevator? How many bags of shopping is she carrying?

  Picture 5: Where is Emma now? She was kind to carry all the shopping up the stairs, but is she tired now? Is Grandpa happy?

Suggested story

Emma is in the street now. Emma is in the supermarket now. She is doing the shopping. Emma is in Grandpa's building again now, but the elevator isn't working. She is carrying lots of bags. She isn't happy. Now she is at Grandpa's apartment. She is tired but her grandpa is happy.

Test tip: FLYERS
Speaking (all parts)

✔ Learners need to complete four tasks. Make sure they are familiar with the order of tasks and what they will need to do, so they feel as confident as possible. They may want to ask the examiner to repeat an instruction. Tell learners it is fine to do that.

→ Practise using greetings and leave-takings and asking for clarification or a repeated instruction, e.g. *Sorry! I don't understand. Sorry! Can you say that again?* Knowing it is fine to talk in this way will reassure learners they will be helped if necessary.

Extension

Learners use these picture prompts to write the story in their notebooks. Walk around and help with vocabulary and grammar if necessary.

Read the text. Choose the right words and write them on the lines.

- Say *Look at the picture. What do you know about eagles? Are there any golden eagles in this country? Where do they live? What do they eat?* (learners answer)

- Learners look at the text, the gaps and possible answers. Ask *How many words do you write for each answer?* (one) *How many words can you choose from?* (three)

- Learners do this as a test task on their own or in pairs to complete the text.

- Check answers in open class.

- Ask *How many kinds of eagles are there?* (60) *Where do eagles build their nests?* (on high hills, mountains or in tall trees in forests) *What colour are their eggs?* (white) *How many colours can they see? A lot or only a few?* (a lot) *How fast can they fly?* (150 kilometres an hour) *What do they eat?* (lizards, mice, fish and other birds)

Answers

2 These **3** build **4** called **5** more **6** to **7** such **8** it

---

Look and remember. Then write a shopping list.

- Say *Look carefully at the picture for one minute.* Then say *Close your books!*

- Ask *What can you remember? Write in your notebooks the things you saw.* In pairs, learners race to write down everything they can remember. They can use dictionaries to find words or check spellings. Pairs put up their hands to show you when they have finished. The winners are the fastest pair with the most correct answers.

- Check answers in open class by looking again at the picture on page 27.

Answers

glue   a necklace   a bracelet   a ring   a ticket
bandage   shampoo   soap   a trainer   a flag
a toothbrush   a letter

Extension

Divide the class into pairs. Say *We're going to play a 'Listen carefully' game! Write a shopping list. Write ten things.* Learners write their list and then work with another pair. Pairs take turns to read out their list twice while the other pair listens and then writes down as many things as they can remember. The winners are the pair who wrote down the most correct words.

Let's have fun!

Make a map of a town centre.

Learners look at the map on page 69 and guess what each building is by looking at the drawings inside the coloured blocks. Learners then read the instructions for drawing their own town maps. Give each learner Photocopy 3 (TB page 56). Learners can imagine a town or draw a map of their own town, thinking of ways to show the different buildings (e.g. a bottle of shampoo to show a chemist's). Learners complete the map including roads and their names, rivers, bridges, traffic lights and bus stops.

Write the word *key* on the board. Say *You use a key to open a …* (door) Explain, in L1, that *key* is also the word for the buttons we press on a computer *keyboard* and information about symbols or different kinds of lines we show on maps.

Learners show what each building is by completing the key under the map.

Let's speak!

Ask and answer about a shop.

Learners look at page 72, Activity 3. Ask two learners to read out the speech bubbles. Ask *Which other shops is the girl going to go to?* Learners guess. Choose two shops and ask *What might she buy there?* Pairs then role play their own conversations. They can write shopping lists and mime carrying bags to put their shopping in.

Ask two or three pairs to role play their conversation in open class.

30

 Let's say!

Say *Look at page 74, Activity 3. Listen.* Play the audio.
Ask *Did you hear the /uː/ sounds in choosing, fruit, juice, glue, shampoo, moved, through, group, kangaroos and supermarket?*
Say each word. Learners repeat in chorus. They could circle the /uː/ sounds on the page.
Learners listen to the rhyme again.
Ask *Who can say this really fast?* Learners repeat the rhyme in chorus.
Say *There's an* /uː/ *sound in 'Who' too. Can you hear it? Can you think of more story words with the sound* /uː/ *in them?* Learners find words in the story. Write their suggestions on the board. (e.g. you, shoe, too, view, huge, flew, Moon, blue)
You could also show learners that *two/too* and *through/ threw* sound exactly the same.

🏠 **Home FUN booklet**

➡ **Pages 2–3 and 16–17 animals; places and directions**
➡ **Picture dictionary: animals; places and buildings**

Go online

to practise your English
to listen to the audio recordings
to find more FUN activities!

A cake for a queen

Main topics:	food, cooking
Story summary:	The unkind queen asks Harry to cook her birthday cake. It must be the best cake she has ever tasted.
Main grammar:	present perfect, *yet*, *still*, *ago*
Main vocabulary:	*ago, anything, appear, begin, break, burn, butter, castle, disappear, enormous, flour, friendly, full, gold, honey, hour, jam, job, kind, later, meal, mix, money, news, oven, pepper, piece, pocket, queen, silver, special, spoon, stone, strawberry, suddenly, sugar, taste, unhappy, unkind, until, usually, whisper, wife*
Value:	Showing kindness (*"This is for you!"*)
Let's say!:	/ɜː/
Practice tasks:	Reading and Writing Part 1 (A), Listening Part 2 (I), Speaking Part 4 (J)
Test tasks:	Reading and Writing Part 4 (G), Listening Part 1 (H)
Equipment:	• audio: Storytelling, H, I, Let's say! • (presentation **PLUS**) flashcards Go to Presentation plus to find pictures of Flyers vocabulary from Unit 4. You can use the pictures to teach/review important words in this unit. • (presentation **PLUS**) Image carousel 15–21 (cake, butter, flour, sugar, milk, eggs, bowl): Storytelling	• Photocopy 4, one per learner (TB page 57): Storytelling Extension • crayons or colouring pencils: Storytelling Extension, Let's have fun! • sheets of plain paper (one per learner): Let's have fun!

Storytelling

Before listening

With books closed …

- Introduce the topic of the story. Ask *Does your family have special cakes on birthdays?* Say *This story is about an unkind queen. She tells her cooks to make a very special birthday cake.* Use the picture on the Image carousel to review/teach *cake*.

- Review/Teach *butter, sugar, flour, eggs* and *milk* using pictures from the Image carousel. Ask *What other things can you put in a cake?* (e.g. chocolate, apples, carrots, coffee, honey) Review/Teach *delicious, enormous* and *special*. Mime eating some cake to teach *delicious*. Say *This tastes great! It's delicious!* Ask *What else is delicious?* Draw a very large cake to teach *enormous*. Say *This cake is so big. It's huge! It's enormous!* Ask *Which animals are enormous?* (learners suggest ideas) Ask *Is your birthday important?* (yes) *Is it different from other days?* (yes) *Your birthday is important, and different from other days, so it's special. Birthday cakes are special cakes too.* Review/Teach *bowl* using the picture on the Image carousel. Remember you can use the flashcards on Presentation plus to help you teach and review vocabulary.

- Look at the first story picture without the story text on the Image carousel or with the story text in the book on page 28. Point to the picture of the bowl. Say *What an enormous bowl!* Say *The cooks work in the queen's castle, but which room is this?* (the kitchen) *How many cooks are there?* (three) *Who else can you see?* (a girl)

- Say *Now let's look at the pictures and listen to the story.* Say *Let's look at page 28.*

Listening

With books open …

▶ Play the audio or read the story. Learners listen.

11 Play the audio or read the story again.

- Pause after *'We can put flour, honey, mangoes and brown sugar in it too!' Matt said* on page 28. Ask *What's the queen's name?* (Alice) *Is she a kind queen?* (no) *What are the cooks' names?* (Harry, Matt, Hugo) *Why must they put 50 different kinds of food in the queen's cake?* (the queen will be 50 years old)

- Pause after *'because we can't get back into the kitchen until we do!'* on page 30. Ask *Who gave Harry the last thing to put in the cake?* (the girl) *What was it?* (a special pear) *Why couldn't the cooks get back into the kitchen?* (it was full of cake) *Did the cake taste delicious?* (yes)

After listening

- After listening to the whole story, ask *Who had to eat lots of cake before Harry could take some to the queen?* (the cooks, their families and all the people in the village) *Was the queen still angry at the end of the story?* (no) *Do you like the ending of the story?* Learners vote *yes* or *no* by putting up their hands. Say *Choose a name for the girl.* Learners suggest ideas and agree on the best. Use the girl's new name where she is mentioned in other activities.

 Value

- In L1, discuss the idea of wanting to help other people and to make them happier. Ask *What good thing did the girl in the wood do? How can you make your family or your friends feel happier?* Brainstorm ideas, e.g. *You can make someone happier by giving them your time, doing a small job for them or giving them a thoughtful present.* Ask *Who is good at making you happier? What do they do? Are you good at thinking of ways to make people happier? Who do you help feel better?* Accept answers in English or L1.

Extension

Ask *Who is a good friend in the story?* (the girl) Give each learner Photocopy 4 (TB page 57). Learners draw (or stick on) a picture of a friend (real or imaginary) and complete the sentences about them. Encourage learners to add their own ideas and to decorate the page.
Display their pages in the classroom if possible.

 A **Read and write the words.**

- Learners look at the sentences. Say *The coloured words are the answers. How many coloured words are there?* (eight) *You can see the example. How many more coloured words do you need for the answers?* (five)

- Learners work on their own or in pairs to match the definitions with their answers. Check answers in open class.

Answers

2 a strawberry **3** honey **4** a castle **5** an oven
6 a wood

Extension

In pairs, learners write definitions for *butter* and *steps*, e.g.
This is usually yellow. People put it on bread, but it isn't cheese.
These are like stairs, but they are usually outside. You can walk up or down them.

 B **Read and circle the correct answer.**

- Write on the board *Queen Alice* and *Harry*. Ask *What describing words* (adjectives) *can you think of for these people in the story?* Learners suggest ideas, e.g. *Queen Alice: unkind, angry, hungry, rich, unfriendly; Harry: poor, hungry, brave, happy.*

- Ask *Is Harry happy at the start of the story?* (no) *Why?* (he's hungry and he has to work hard) *Is his job at the castle easy?* (no) *How does he feel at the end of the story?* (happy, brave, not frightened)

- Learners look at Activity B. Ask *Was Queen Alice always nice or never kind before her birthday?* (never kind) *So the circle is around 'never kind'. Now you read and circle the right answers.*

- Learners work on their own to circle the answers. They can find answers by checking in the story. Check answers in open class.

- Ask *Have you ever drunk rain water / made a delicious cake / met a king or queen?*

Answers

2 really poor **3** young girl **4** rain water **5** More than
6 quite brave

 C **Put the words in order. Write the conversation.**

- Learners look at the word box and the picture. Ask *Who are these people?* (the girl and Harry) Say *The girl gave Harry a pear. What did the girl say? What was Harry's answer?* Make two sentences with the words in the box.

- Learners complete the speech bubbles. Check answers.

Answers

This is for you!
Thank you very much!

- In L1 if necessary, ask learners again about the message of this story. Ask *What did the girl do to help the cooks?* (she gave them the pear) *What will Queen Alice do to make her cooks feel happier in the future?* (learners suggest ideas)

- In small groups, learners discuss and plan five charitable things to do to make five different people happier this month. Say that one of these five good deeds should happen without the person knowing who did it.

- Suggestions: Learners could write a letter or make a cake for a parent or grandparent. They could help a cousin or younger brother/sister with their homework. They could leave some flowers on a neighbour's doorstep.

- Review/Teach *You're welcome.*

  Write on the board:

  A: This is for you!

  B: Thank you very much!

  A: You're welcome.

  Ask two learners to come to the front of the class to mime giving and receiving something and to role play the conversation.

Extension

Brainstorm other objects or small presents that friends might give each other. Write the ideas that learners suggest on the board, e.g. *a biscuit, a pencil case, a comic, some chocolate.* In pairs, learners choose presents to give and then role play the conversation again in closed pairs. They can add a third and fourth turn, e.g. *You're welcome! / No problem! / I love it! It's fantastic/beautiful/amazing/delicious!*

D Look at the picture on page 28. Read and write *yes* or *no*.

- Say *Look at the picture on page 28. Find as many things as you can that begin with the letter c.* Learners list words in pairs. Give them a few minutes before asking *Has anyone found more than five? More than eight? More than ten?*

- Pairs take turns to make two suggestions each. When you are checking the words, you could ask *What else?* Write learners' suggestions on the board, e.g. *carrots, castle, chair, chicken, child, clock, clothes, coat, cook, cooker, corner, cupboard.*

- Review/Teach *burn, finger* and *right hand* using the picture on page 28 and mime. Ask a learner to mime burning their finger. Ask *Does that hurt?* Teach *pocket* by miming putting an object in a pocket. Ask *Have you got pockets in your clothes today? What do you keep in your pockets?*

- Learners look at the example in Activity D and the picture on page 28. Ask *Why is this answer 'no'?* (there are only two biscuits on the plate) Learners read the sentences and write *yes* or *no* after each one.

- Check answers in open class. Learners could correct the false sentences.

Answers

2 yes   3 no   4 yes   5 no   6 yes   7 yes

Extension

Pairs choose another picture and write four sentences (two right, two wrong) about it. Pairs then swap sentences and write *yes* or *no* next to each sentence.

E What have or haven't they done? Write the correct form of the verb.

- Review/Teach *yet* and the irregular past participles of *bring (brought), give (given)* and *put (put).*

- Say *Look at the picture in Activity E. What's on the table?* Learners answer. Say *The cooks have put 49 different kinds of food in the bowl, but we can only see some of them.*

- Learners look at the example. Ask *Has Harry put any eggs in the bowl yet?* (yes, he has) *Has he put the pear in yet?* (no, he hasn't) *Has he put the chocolate in yet?* (no, he hasn't)

- Write on the board *Harry has broken lots of eggs into the bowl.* Ask *Why is the first word 'has'?* (because we say *Harry has,* not *Harry have*) Say *We say 'Harry (he) has' and 'Harry and John (they) have'.*

- In pairs, learners write the missing words in 2–6 in the gaps. Check answers in open class.

- Ask *Is the table tidy or untidy?* (untidy) *Are Harry, Matt and Hugo tidy cooks?* (no) *Are you a tidy person?*

Answers

2 haven't added   3 has brought   4 has given
5 has put   6 haven't cleaned

F Complete the sentences with *ago, yet* or *still*.

- Review/Teach *ago, yet* and *still*. Write the words on the board. Say *Which word can we use to talk about something that was happening before and is happening*

now too? 'Yet' or 'still'? (still) *Which word can we use to talk about something that hasn't happened?* (yet)

- Point to the words on the board again. Ask *Which word can mean 'before now' or 'in the past'?* (ago) Ask *How old were you two years ago?* (learners answer)

- Learners look at both pictures. Ask *Are the two pictures the same or different?* (the same) Ask *Where was the queen two days ago?* (in her room) *Where is she now?* (in her room) *Has she left her room yet?* (no) *The queen is still in her room.*

- Write the sentence *She hasn't left her room yet* on the board. Say *In this sentence, where is 'yet'? In the middle or at the end of the sentence?* (the end) *'Yet' usually comes at the end of the sentence.*

- Learners read sentences 2–6 and complete them with the right word. They can compare their answers in pairs before checking in open class.

Answers

2 yet   3 ago   4 still   5 ago   6 still

G Read the text. Choose the right words and write them on the lines.

- Learners look at the picture. Ask *What's this?* (a cake) Say *It looks good. Do you think it tastes good too?* (learners give their opinions)

- Say *Write down as many things as you can that were in the queen's cake!* In groups of three, without looking at the story, learners try to remember the ingredients that went into the queen's cake. Make this a race.

- Write all 15 ingredients on the board when you check their answers. (eggs, strawberry jam, butter, milk, flour, honey, mangoes, brown sugar, kiwi juice, apples, coffee, carrots, chocolate, pepper, a pear)

- Learners look at the text and answers. Ask *What do you have to do?* (choose the right word for each gap) *Where are the missing words?* (next to the text)

- Learners work on their own to complete the text. Check answers by asking different learners to read out each sentence. Ask their classmates *Do you agree with that answer?*

Answers

1 they   2 which   3 ago   4 still   5 not   6 making
7 called   8 all   9 Have   10 someone

Test tip: FLYERS
Reading and Writing (Part 4)

✔ Learners read a factual text and choose which word (from three possible answers) should go in the grammatical gap. Only one word is correct.

→ Use three or four lines from any story text and remove key grammatical words, e.g. *if, while, much, than, so, during, just, quite, each,* and ask learners to guess which word might fit. Accept any possible answers.

Extension

Learners write three true or false sentences about cakes. Their partner says *That's right/wrong!*

H Listen and draw lines.

- Ask *Do you have a garden? What can you see or do in your garden / a garden? Do you grow vegetables?*

- Write *garden* on the board vertically and ask learners in pairs to add words horizontally to it. The words should be things you can see in a garden or vegetable garden, e.g.

```
        g r a s  s
    p l a n t  s
        r a b b i t
  b i r d s
      t r e e
  b e a n s
```

- Learners look at the picture in Activity H. Ask *What's happening in this garden?* Learners describe what they can see and what people are doing. Ask *Can you see anyone from the story?* (Harry, Hugo, Matt)
- Say *Listen to the girl. She's going to tell someone the names of the people in this vegetable garden.*

12

- Play the audio and pause after the example. Point to the line between *Richard* and the boy. Ask *What did the girl tell us about Richard?* (He's between the puppy and the fire. He's found some carrots.)
- Play the rest of the audio. Learners listen and draw lines between the names and the other people in the picture. Play the audio again. Learners check their answers in pairs.
- Ask *Which names didn't you hear?* (Harry, Matt) Ask *Where's Harry in this picture? What's he doing?* (walking to the door) *Where's Matt? What's he doing?* (sitting on the chair)
- In pairs, learners write similar mini-conversations to identify Harry and Matt in the picture. Ask three or four pairs to role play their conversation in open class.

A: *Who's that man near the door?*

B: *That's Harry.*

A: *What's he doing?*

B: *He's going to look at the cake.*

Tapescript:

Listen and look. There is one example.

Man: Who are all these people in the vegetable garden?

Girl: Well, that boy is called Richard.

Man: Do you mean the boy between the puppy and the fire?

Girl: That's right. The one who's found some carrots.

Can you see the line? This is an example. Now you listen and draw lines.

Man: Who else is here?

Girl: One of the cooks. There! With his knees on the ground. That's Hugo.

Man: Oh! He hasn't finished his work yet. There's still lots to do!

Girl: Yes, but he's already done quite a lot of planting.

Man: Does that person work in the castle as well?

Girl: The woman who's putting the clothes on the line? Yes! That's Sophia.

Man: Why has she got a fork in her pocket?

Girl: I don't know!

Girl: There's Michael! He's planted all those beans.

Man: Which one's he?

Girl: The man with dirty hands and with his arms in the air.

Man: Oh, yes!

Man: And who's that? The one with gloves on?

Girl: Do you mean the girl with curly hair?

Man: No. The one with straight hair. She's burning the leaves.

Girl: Oh, that's Sarah.

Girl: Can you see the person who's standing near the wood?

Man: The man behind the wood?

Girl: Not him. The person who's cutting the wood. She's got a scarf on her head.

Man: Oh, yes! Who's that?

Girl: She's called Helen.

Man: Great!

Answers

Hugo – knees on ground, planting
Sophia – putting clothes on line, fork in pocket
Michael – dirty hands, arms in air
Sarah – straight hair, wearing gloves, burning leaves
Helen – cutting wood, scarf on head

Test tip: FLYERS
Listening (Part 1)

✔ Learners will see four names above the picture and three names below the picture. These names are likely to come from the Flyers word list. Learners will need to draw lines between five of these names to people in the picture to complete the task (one is also given as an example). Make sure learners know the 16 Flyers names and whether they are used to name boys/men or girls/women.

➜ Teach learners the complete list of Flyers names and use them frequently in any other lesson activities.

Flyers names:

For boys: David, Frank, George, Harry, Michael, Oliver, Richard, Robert, William

For girls: Betty, Emma, Helen, Holly, Katy, Sarah, Sophia

Extension

Learners work in groups to write a poem using the letters from ***garden*** vertically to form one word in each line, e.g.

*I'm **g**oing into my garden.*

* **A**re you coming too?*

*We can pick flowe**r**s.*

* Or **d**raw something blue.*

*I lov**e** my garden.*

* A**n**d you do, don't you?*

Walk around and help with ideas and vocabulary. Ask some groups to read out their poem in open class.

I Listen and write Robert's answers. Write one word.

- Ask *What do you like eating for breakfast?* Write learners' answers on the board.
- Say *You're going to hear a boy called Robert. He's talking about food.*
- Learners look at the questions and example. Ask *How many words must you write?* (one)

13

- Play the audio twice. Learners listen and write the answers.
- Ask *What were Robert's answers?* Ask each question. Learners answer.

Answers

2 grandma **3** kitchen **4** pizza **5** apple

Tapescript:

Listen and look. There is one example.

Woman:	Hello, Robert! Let's talk about food. What do you like eating for breakfast?
Boy:	Oh, I really enjoy eating eggs. I love having those for breakfast.
Woman:	Do you?
Boy:	Yes!

Can you see the answer? Now you listen and write.

Woman:	And who cooks the meals in your home?
Boy:	My grandma. She's a great cook. She makes really delicious cakes!
Woman:	You're lucky then! Where do you eat your meals? Have you got a dining room?
Boy:	Yes, we have, but we usually eat in the kitchen. We've got a big table in it, so everyone can sit there together.
Woman:	That's good. Tell me about the food you often eat, then.
Boy:	Oh … I love yoghurts. I often have one after my lunch. And my favourite dinner is pizza.
Woman:	OK. What food don't you like?
Boy:	I don't like mangoes or olives.
Woman:	All right. And do you ever take a snack with you to eat at school? Some biscuits, for example?
Boy:	No, apples usually. Those are better for me, my mum says.
Woman:	Right! Well, thanks for answering my questions.
Boy:	That's OK.

J Talk about food and then answer for you.

- Divide learners into pairs or small groups. Say *Look at the sentences and talk about answers with your friend. Then complete the sentences. You can write as many words as you want.* Walk around and help with vocabulary if necessary.
- Pairs take turns to feed back their answers to the class.

Test tip: FLYERS
Speaking (Part 4)

- ✔ Learners need to be able to answer simple questions about themselves.
- → Make sure learners can answer simple questions about, e.g. their age, their hobbies, their likes and dislikes, their friends, their home, what they like doing at the weekend, their favourite animals/colours/sports, how they travel to school.

Extension

Ask *What is the most popular food in this class?* The class suggest ideas and vote for their favourite foods. They can draw and illustrate a simple bar chart in their notebooks.

4

Let's have fun!

Read, then write your recipe. Draw pictures.

Learners look at the information in Activity 4 on page 69. Ask *Have you ever entered a competition like this?* (learners answer) Learners plan their recipe, making notes in their notebooks. Give each learner a sheet of paper. Learners write their recipe and add a drawing and instructions to make their special cake. Walk around and help with ideas and vocabulary if necessary. When learners have finished, they take turns to talk about their recipe. Ask *Would you like to make this special cake at home?*

4

Let's speak!

Invent information about the girl in the story. Ask and answer.

Learners look at page 72, Activity 4. Brainstorm answers to the questions in open class. In pairs, learners then ask and answer these questions and a few others about the girl in the story. They could then write a 'question and answer interview' about the girl in their notebooks.

31

Let's say!

Say *Look at page 74, Activity 4. Listen.* Play the audio. Ask *Did you hear the /ɜː/ sounds in thirty, were, working, circle, perfect, birthday, world?*
Say each word. Learners repeat in chorus. They could circle the /ɜː/ sounds on the page.
Learners listen to the rhyme again.
Ask *Who can say these words really fast?* Learners repeat the rhyme in chorus.
Say *There's an /ɜː/ sound in 'words' too. Can you hear it? Can you think of more story words with the sound /ɜː/ in them?* Learners find words in the story. Write their suggestions on the board. (e.g. girl, her, answered, whispered, early, curly, dirty, first)

🏠 Home FUN booklet

- ➡ **Pages 8–9 and 30–31 food and drink; adjectives**
- ➡ **Picture dictionary: food and drink**

Go online

to practise your English
to listen to the audio recordings
to find more FUN activities!

Katy's favourite song

5

Main topics:	music
Story summary:	Katy loves music, especially her favourite pop star Alex Pepper. One day he comes to her school to listen to their music competition.
Main grammar:	*will, going to, ask somebody to do something,* present perfect
Main vocabulary:	*belt, competition, drums, gloves, instruments, manager, prize, stadium, stage, violin, winner*
Value:	Encouraging your friends and others (*"Don't worry." "Come on!"*)
Let's say!:	/eɪ/
Practice tasks:	Reading and Writing Part 1 (A), Reading and Writing Part 5 (B), Listening Part 5 (F)
Test tasks:	Listening Part 2 (G), Speaking Part 2 (I)

Equipment:

- ▶ audio: Storytelling, F, G, J, Let's say!

- ↪ (presentation **PLUS**) flashcards

  Go to Presentation plus to find pictures of Flyers vocabulary from Unit 5. You can use the pictures to teach/ review important words in this unit.

- ↪ (presentation **PLUS**) Image carousel 22–34

  (poster, prize, music competition; trainers, gloves, pocket, belt, jacket, shoes, scarf, socks, shorts, top): Storytelling; E

- Photocopy 5, one per learner (TB page 58): Storytelling Extension
- necklace and bracelet (optional): F
- sheets of plain paper (one per learner), magazines, scissors, glue: Let's have fun!
- crayons or colouring pencils: Storytelling Extension, E Extension, F, Let's have fun!, Let's speak!

 Storytelling

Before listening

With books closed …

- Introduce the topic of the story. Ask *Do you like listening to music? Can any of you play an instrument? Which instrument might you like to learn to play?* (the drums/piano/guitar/violin) *Do you ever watch music competitions on television? Would you like to be in a music competition one day? Is it scary to stand on a stage and sing or play an instrument?* Say *This story is about a girl and a boy who are in a music competition.*

- Review/Teach *pop star* and *practise.* Remember you can use the flashcards on Presentation plus to help you teach and review vocabulary. Use the Image carousel to review/teach *music competition, poster* and *prize.* Ask *Do you have any posters of pop stars in your room at home? Which ones? If you win a music competition, someone might give you a prize! Which is the best kind of prize? Tickets to a festival, a concert or the cinema?* Say *If you want to get better at playing an instrument or your favourite sport, it's important to practise very often. What do you practise doing?*

- Look at the first story picture without the story text on the Image carousel or with the story text in the book on page 36. Ask *What subject do students learn in this classroom?* (music) *How many instruments can you see?* (three) *How many students are in the classroom at the moment?* (two) Say *Their names are Katy and Paul. Are they the same age?* (learners guess) *What are they going to do next?* (learners guess)

- Say *Now let's look at the pictures and listen to the story.* Say *Let's look at page 36.*

Listening

With books open …

14

- Play the audio or read the story. Learners listen.
- Play the audio or read the story again.
- Pause after *He wanted to be the coolest guitar player in the world* on page 36. Ask *Do the friends like going away on holiday or going to school?* (going to school) *What does Katy want to be one day?* (a pop star) *Which instruments can she play?* (the piano, the violin) *Who is good at English?* (Paul)
- Pause after *'You're next!' called Mr White and pointed to Paul and Katy* on page 38. Ask *Who is Mr White?* (Katy and Paul's teacher) *How often did the two friends practise for the competition?* (every afternoon) *Who is going to choose the winner of the competition?* (Alex Pepper) *How are Katy and Paul feeling now? Will they win the competition?* (learners guess)

After listening

- After listening to the whole story, ask *Which song did they sing and play?* ('I'm your friend') *Was it amazing or really bad?* (amazing) *What did Katy and Paul win?* (tickets to Alex Pepper's concert)
- Ask *Was the concert in a theatre or at a stadium?* (a stadium) *Will Katy and Paul be famous (like Alex Pepper) one day?* (learners guess) *Would you like to be a famous pop star, or do you prefer rock music?*

Value

- In L1 if necessary, talk about the friendship between Paul and Katy. Ask *Is Paul a good friend? Why? How did he make it easier for Katy to sing well in the competition? What did he say to encourage her?* ('It'll sound wonderful!' 'Don't worry. You're brilliant, Katy. We'll sing this together! Come on!') Ask *Do you think it's important to encourage other people? Do you sometimes encourage a younger brother or sister? When you aren't feeling brave or clever enough to do something, how does it feel when someone encourages you to do it? Does it make you want to try? Why? / Why not?* Learners answer. Reassure learners that they won't always be able to do different things and that this is OK. We are all different and good at some things and not so good at others and that's fine.

Extension

Give each learner Photocopy 5 (TB page 58). Learners look at the story competition poster and choose words to complete it.

In pairs, learners can use this poster as a model to help them design another competition poster, e.g. for a photography competition, a cookery competition or an art competition. Learners choose all the details. Encourage them to add decorations or drawings. Walk around and help with ideas or vocabulary if necessary. Display the posters around the room if possible.

A Read and complete the words.

- Say *We need to complete these spellings.* Learners look at the example. Ask *What's the word?* (concert)
- Learners work on their own to complete the spellings of the other words. If necessary, learners check their spellings by finding the words in the story.
- Check answers. Ask different learners to spell one of the words.

Answers

2 stage 3 drums 4 Instruments
5 violin 6 stadium

B Read and answer questions. Write 1, 2, 3 or 4 words.

- Learners look at the example. Ask *What does Mr White teach?* (music) Ask *How many words can you write in these answers?* (one, two, three or four)
- Learners work in pairs to answer the questions from memory if they can and then check their answers in the story.
- Check answers in open class. Ask more questions: *Where did Katy and Paul practise?* (in Katy's basement) *Who went to the concert with Paul?* (his sisters and George) *What kind of pet has Katy got?* (a parrot)

Answers

2 I'll help you! 3 I'm your friend 4 (very) alone and afraid 5 City Stadium 6 (her/Katy's) aunt and cousins

Extension

In pairs, learners write three or four more questions about the story for other pairs to answer.

C This is one of Katy's friends. Choose answers to the questions.

- In L1, explain that learners can invent answers to these questions. Ask *What's this girl's name?* (learners guess) Encourage a range of suggestions. Say *Now read and answer the other questions.* Learners do this creative thinking task in pairs.
- Different pairs feed back one of their answers in open class.
- In L1 if necessary, ask learners again about the message of this story. Then, using the chosen girl's name in Activity C, ask *How can you help (Rosa) to feel less frightened or worried?* Accept all valid answers.
- Ask, in L1 if necessary, *Why is it so scary to stand on a stage in front of lots of people? If you had to do this, what could you do to feel braver? How can you help someone in your family or one of your best friends to do well or feel braver when they are frightened or worried?*

D It's Thursday afternoon. What is Katy going to do? What has she already done?

- Say *Look at the picture. Who is practising on the piano?* (Katy) *Which day is she doing that?* (Thursday)
- Review *going to*, and *already* + present perfect. Ask *What day is it now?* (e.g. Monday) *What day is it going to be tomorrow?* (e.g. Tuesday) Ask two or three learners *What have you done earlier today? You have …* (had breakfast / come to school / played volleyball) Say *So you can say you have already had breakfast / come to school / played volleyball.*
- Learners look at the example. Ask *Does Katy know all the words to Alex's best songs now?* (yes) *Did she learn them earlier?* (yes) Say *So Katy can say 'I have already learned all the words to Alex's songs.'*
- Learners work in pairs and complete Katy's speech bubbles using a word in the box in the correct form.

Answers

2 am going to wait 3 have already listened 4 am going to practise 5 have already invited 6 am going to take

E Look, read and draw lines.

- Review/Teach *trainers, gloves, pocket, belt, jacket, shoes, scarf, socks, shorts* and *top*, using the Image carousel. Ask *What are you wearing today?*

- Say *Look at the pictures. What clothes are these?* (accept all valid answers) Say *On the day of the competition, Alex wore a black …* (jacket) *How many pockets are there on the black jacket here?* (two) Review/Teach *spotted* and *striped* by drawing spots and stripes on the board. Ask *Is the scarf spotted or striped?* (striped)
- Learners match the clothes and the words. Walk around and check while learners draw their lines.
- Ask *Are the trainers green or pink?* (pink) *What colour is the belt?* (yellow and orange) *Which clothes keep your hands and your neck warm?* (the gloves and scarf) Ask three or four learners *What are your favourite clothes?*

Answers

A my coolest shorts   **B** some funny shoes   **C** a striped scarf   **D** some warm gloves   **E** a jacket with pockets   **F** a spotted top   **G** my new trainers   **H** my striped belt   **I** a pair of socks

Extension

Learners design, draw and label clothes for themselves to wear on a special day. Brainstorm ideas in open class. Ask *What would you like to wear to a really cool party / at a sports competition / on a beach or mountain holiday?* On their own or in small groups, learners choose a special day, design and draw their clothes and add a description of their outfit. Learners could present their designs in open class.

F Look at the picture on page 38. Listen and colour and write.

- Review/Teach *necklace* and *bracelet* by showing learners these if possible. Learners look at the picture on page 38. Say *Katy and Paul are on the stage.*
- Ask *What is Katy wearing?* (a skirt, a T-shirt, a belt, a bracelet, some shoes) *What is Paul wearing?* (a T-shirt, jeans, socks, shoes) *What has someone already coloured green?* (Katy's belt)
- Say *You are going to colour some of the clothes in this picture and write some words.* Make sure learners have their colouring pencils or crayons.

15
- Play the audio twice.
- Check answers in open class. Learners should try to answer in full sentences, e.g. *What colour is Paul's top?* (Paul's top is orange.)

Answers

Paul's top – orange
Katy's skirt pockets – blue
Katy's bracelet – purple
Write 'drums' on box behind Katy
Write 'clap' above 'loudly' in circle behind Paul

Tapescript:

Listen and look at the picture. There is one example.

Man:	Would you like to colour some parts of this picture?
Girl:	Sure! Can I colour Katy's belt first, please?
Man:	Yes. Colour it green.
Girl:	OK. There. I've done that.

Can you see Katy's green belt? This is an example. Now you listen and colour and write.

1 Man: Let's colour Paul's top next. You can choose the colour for that.

Girl: I'd like to colour that orange.

Man: All right! Is that your favourite colour?

Girl: It's one of my favourites.

2 Girl: I'd like to colour the pockets on Katy's skirt. Can I do that now?

Man: Of course! Colour those blue. They'll look good that colour.

Girl: I agree! I'll do that now.

Man: Thank you.

3 Girl: Can I write something here as well? Perhaps on the circle above the star?

Man: Actually, I'd like you to write on the big box behind Katy instead.

Girl: OK. What shall I write there?

Man: 'Drums'. It's where they keep the largest ones.

Girl: Fine.

4 Man: Katy's wearing a big bracelet. Could you also colour that?

Girl: Yes. But I can't decide on the colour … What about yellow?

Man: I think purple will look better. Make it that colour, please.

Girl: OK!

5 Man: This picture needs some more writing on it, actually.

Girl: Does it? On the circle this time?

Man: Yes. Have you got your pencil ready?

Girl: Yes!

Man: Great! Write the word 'Clap' above the word 'loudly'!

Girl: Ha ha! Good idea. All right.

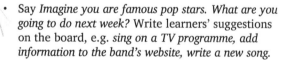

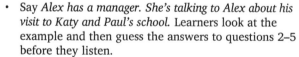

G Listen and write.

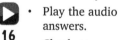

- Say *Imagine you are famous pop stars. What are you going to do next week?* Write learners' suggestions on the board, e.g. *sing on a TV programme, add information to the band's website, write a new song.*
- Say *Alex has a manager. She's talking to Alex about his visit to Katy and Paul's school.* Learners look at the example and then guess the answers to questions 2–5 before they listen.

16
- Play the audio twice. Learners listen and write their answers.
- Check answers in open class. Ask *Does Alex's manager like his trainers?* (no) *Why?* (because they are old and grey) *Does Alex think his manager is good at her job?* (yes)

Answers

1 Burtly   **2** 1.30   **3** silver   **4** sunglasses   **5** 088659112

Tapescript:

Woman:	Hi, Alex. How are you?
Man:	Great, thanks! What am I going to do this week?
Woman:	Well, you're going to go to a music competition one afternoon.
Man:	Am I? Which day is that?
Woman:	Thursday. That's the 23rd of May. The same day as your concert.

Can you see the answer? Now you listen and write.

Man:	Where is this competition?
Woman:	It's at Burtly School.
Man:	Oh, yes. I remember. The teacher there phoned you about it. Do you spell that B-U-R-T-L-Y?
Woman:	Yes, that's right. The school has a website. It's easy to find on the internet if you're interested.
Man:	OK.
Woman:	Now your driver is going to come to collect you from your hotel at one forty-five … sorry, that's wrong, at one thirty. Please be ready.
Man:	No problem! I'll wear my usual clothes and …
Woman:	You must wear your silver boots, Alex. Not those old grey trainers!
Man:	OK.
Woman:	And don't forget to take some sunglasses too.
Man:	All right! I won't. Can you give me the teacher's phone number? I don't want any problems.
Woman:	Sure. It's here on his message. His name is Mr White and his number is zero, double eight, six, five, nine, double one, two. I sent him ten tickets to give as prizes.
Man:	Fantastic! Thanks, Emma. You're an amazing manager!
Woman:	I know! Now have you written all that information in your diary?
Man:	Yes! Don't worry.

Test tip: FLYERS
Listening (Part 2)

✔ Learners listen to a conversation that is often about some kind of event. The conversation might contain a number (e.g. a date), a name which is spelled out, and other pieces of information about the event. Learners complete a form with short answers (usually one word or a number). Sometimes part of an answer is given before or after the gap on the form, e.g.
Date: _____ March
Teacher's name: Mr _____

➔ Learners could create fact files for different events, e.g. a school trip, a visit to a chocolate factory, a trip to a rock concert, a birthday party. They list prompts (and answers), e.g. *Date: Time: Name: Address: Take: How get there:*

Extension

Learners imagine they are someone famous, e.g. a film star, a sports player, an astronaut. They make a diary page showing the days of the week. They write notes about what they are going to do each day. Learners should use fun ideas, e.g. *Monday: Have a meeting with the costume designer and then dinner with the queen.*

H What will the friends do before the concert? What will you do? Talk and write.

- Ask *Who's talking on the telephones?* (Katy's two cousins) Say *They are talking about things they want to do before they go to the concert.*

- Divide the class into groups of four. In L1, tell learners to imagine they are going to go to a pop concert this evening. Ask *What will you do before the concert? Think of things that will make the evening really wonderful.* Each learner thinks of two things. Learners then write their two *I'll* sentences on the dotted lines.

- Ask different learners to read out their completed speech bubble.

I Ask and answer about the concerts.

- Learners look at the picture of Alex's band. Ask *What instruments did they play at that concert?* (guitars, drums) Say *We're going to talk about Alex's concert and another pop star's. His name is Dan.*

- Learners work in pairs, asking and answering the questions to do this as a test task, or continue with support as follows.

- Learners look at the question prompts. Expand these on the board: **Where** is the **concert**? **What** is the **date**? **What time** does it **start**? **What** does **he play**? What **can** you **buy** there?

- Divide the class into A and B pairs. Learner B turns their book upside down. Learner A asks the questions. Learner B answers about Dan's concert. Then Learner B asks the questions and Learner A answers about Alex's concert. Walk around and help if necessary.

- Feed back in open class, asking the questions and further questions, e.g. *How do you spell 'keyboard'?*

Test tip: FLYERS
Speaking (Part 2)

✔ Learners see five pieces of information about two different situations. These might be about two places, people, pets, presents, parties, etc. Learners give the answers to the examiner's questions about their situation and then ask questions about the examiner's situation. There are prompts to help them form questions, e.g. *Where/concert, Time/start.* Learners use these words to form their questions: **Where** is the **concert**? What **time** does it **start**?

➔ Invent a situation in open class about, e.g. a school trip. Write similar prompts (and chosen answers) on the board. For the prompts, use words in the form and order that learners will need to use in their questions. In pairs, learners ask and answer questions.

J Listen and write the words.

- Review/Teach *if*. Say *If Katy remembers the words, she* <u>*can*</u> *sing her song. If Katy can't remember the words, she* <u>*can't*</u> ... (sing her song) Write on the board *If I want to talk to my best friend, I phone her.* Say *But if I don't want to talk to my best friend, I don't ...* (phone her)

- In L1, show learners that *if* here means the same as *when*. Write unfinished sentences on the board. In pairs, learners think of ways to complete them, e.g.

  If I'm tired, I ...   *If I'm feeling sad, I ...*

  If you're hungry, you can ...   *If you feel bored, play ...*

- Review/Teach *alone*. Write *alone* on the board. Erase *al* so learners see the word *one*. Five learners stand together in a group. Say *You are with your friends.* Then gently guide one learner away from the group. Say to the group *You are still with your friends, but here* (looking at the single learner) *there is only one person. She/He is alone.*

- Divide the class into five groups. Each group looks at one of the five verses of Katy's song. Say *Guess the missing word.*

- Groups choose a word and take turns to read out their verse in chorus.

17

- Play the audio. Ask *Was your missing word the same?* Check answers in open class.

- Ask *When do you like being alone? When do you like being with friends?* Discuss in open class, in L1 if necessary. Learners could then write their two answers on the line under the questions or in their notebooks.

> **Tapescript:**
> See SB and Answers
>
>

> **Answers**
> **2** sad   **3** walk   **4** bad   **5** games

36

> **Extension**
> In their groups, learners learn the song and create actions or a dance routine to accompany the song, which they can perform for the class. You can also play a version of the song without the words for learners to sing along to.

5 Let's have fun!

Write a fact file about your favourite band.

Learners look at page 70, Activity 5. Ask different learners about their favourite band using prompts in the fact file, e.g. *What are the names of the people in your favourite band?* Give each learner a sheet of paper. Learners write a fact file with information about their favourite band (real or imagined). To illustrate their file, learners can cut out pictures from magazines, print them from the internet or draw their own pictures. Display the fact files around the classroom if possible.

5 Let's speak!

Ask and answer. Then draw your favourite instrument.

Learners look at page 73, Activity 5. Ask different learners *Do you like listening to music? Can you play any instruments? Where do you listen to music? What's your favourite instrument?* Learners then talk about listening to music in pairs and draw their favourite instruments in their notebooks.

32

> **Let's say!**
>
> Say *Look at page 75, Activity 5. Listen.* Play the audio. Ask *Did you hear the /eɪ/ sounds in Katy, waited, café, rain, today, amazing, grey, whale, eight, great?*
> Say each word. Learners repeat in chorus. They could circle the /eɪ/ sounds on the page.
> Learners listen to the rhyme again.
> Say *Let's say this rhyme today!* Learners repeat the rhyme in chorus.
> Say *There's an /eɪ/ sound in 'today' too. Can you hear it? Can you think of more story words with the sound /eɪ/ in them?* Learners find words in the story. Write their suggestions on the board. (e.g. holidays, places, stay, player, stage, basement, waved, afraid, stadium)

>   **Home FUN booklet**
>
> → **Pages 4–5 and 18–19 clothes; sports and leisure**
> → **Picture dictionary: clothes; sports and leisure**

> **Go online**
>
> to practise your English
> to listen to the audio recordings
> to find more FUN activities!

William's strangest story

Main topics:	school, home, materials
Story summary:	William is always late. One day he is running to school and falls over. When he wakes up, he is in an alien spaceship.
Main grammar:	*What's it for? It's for …*
Main vocabulary:	*art, dictionary, finger, geography, history, language, late, maths, music, planets, problem, science, scissors, screen, space, Spanish, uniform, wool*
Value:	Remaining calm
Let's say!:	/əʊ/
Practice tasks:	Reading and Writing Part 1 (A), Reading and Writing Part 2 (D), Speaking Part 1 (I)
Test tasks:	Listening Part 3 (E), Reading and Writing Part 3 (G)

Equipment:	• audio: Storytelling, C, E, Let's say! • (presentation **PLUS**) flashcards Go to Presentation plus to find pictures of Flyers vocabulary from Unit 6. You can use the pictures to teach/review important words in this unit. • (presentation **PLUS**) Image carousel 35–37 (Earth, Moon, spaceship): Storytelling	• Photocopy 6A, one per learner (TB page 59): Storytelling Extension • Photocopy 6B, one per learner, cut into a set of cards for each pair (TB page 60): F Extension • coat hanger, card, string or wool, glue or sticky tape and paint for each learner: Let's have fun!

Storytelling

Before listening

With books closed …

- Introduce the topic of the story by talking about space travel. Ask *Would you like to travel to another planet one day? Some people say they see spaceships. Do you believe that?* Say *This story is about a boy called William who meets an alien inside a spaceship!*

- Review/Teach *Earth, Moon* and *spaceship* using the pictures on the Image carousel. Say *Our planet is called Earth.* Write *spaceship* on the board. Say *We make this word by putting 'space' and 'ship' together.* Ask *Would you like to explore space in a spaceship one day? Do you like doing exciting things? Do you like reading about adventures?* Remember you can use the flashcards on Presentation plus to help you teach and review vocabulary.

- Look at the first story picture without the story text on the Image carousel or with the story text in the book on page 44. Ask *Where are these students?* (at school) *Which boy is William?* (learners guess) *What time is it?* (five past nine) *Why is the teacher pointing to the clock?* (William is late) *What are the other children doing?* (laughing)

- Say *Now let's listen to the story.* Say *Let's look at page 44.*

Listening

With books open …

▶ Play the audio or read the story. Learners listen.

18 Play the audio or read the story again.

- Pause after *'today I'm going to be really late for school!'* on page 45. Ask *Why was William often late for school?* (he liked staying in bed) *What happened while William was running to school?* (he fell over) *And where is William now?* (in a spaceship)

- Pause after *'Without a map, it might take much more time to get to school'* on page 46. Ask *Which two things has William shown the alien?* (his dictionary and scissors) *How did the alien learn to speak English?* (it ate William's dictionary) *Why was the alien angry?* (William cut up its space map) *Will William get back to Earth school?* (learners guess)

After listening

- After listening to the whole story, ask *Why couldn't the alien move? What stopped it?* (William's glue and ball of wool) *Where was William at the end of the story?* (in his classroom at school) *Did the teacher believe his story?* (no)

- Discuss in L1 the importance of trying to stay calm when you have a problem. Ask *Why is being calm important?* You could explain that when we are angry it is much harder to think of solutions to problems.
- Ask *What can you do to keep calm when you have a problem?* Learners make suggestions, e.g. count to 10, think positively, ask for help.

Extension

Give each learner Photocopy 6A (TB page 59). Ask *What time do you get up in the morning? Who gets up first in your family? What do you do next? What do you have for breakfast? How do you get to school?*
Learners look at the line through *up* in the word box and at the example. Say *Now you choose one word to complete each sentence.* Learners work in pairs. When they have completed the sentences, check answers and then ask *Did William do all these things in the story?* Learners decide in pairs which sentences are right and then say why the other sentences are wrong. They could add ticks or crosses to show their answers. Check answers in open class.

Answers

1 on ✗ **2** over ✓ **3** off ✗ **4** up ✓ **5** off ✗ **6** for ✗

- Ask *Which other things can you turn on or turn off?* (e.g. a TV, a lamp, a light, a radio, a laptop, a tablet, a computer, a phone, an oven)

 A **Read and write. Then complete the crossword.**

- Ask *What might you see in space?* (e.g. planets, moons, stars, the space station, spaceships, an alien!)
- Learners look at the crossword. Ask *How many answers are already here?* (three) *How many more must you add?* (seven)
- Learners write the answers in the sentences and then add them to the puzzle on their own. They then compare answers in pairs. Check answers in open class. Pairs take turns to read out a completed clue, spelling the answer out loud.

Answers

2 problem **3** scissors **4** English
5 screen **6** history **7** fingers **8** planets

 B **Read and circle the correct answer.**

- Ask *Was William usually early or late for school?* (late) *Are you ever late for school? Why? / Why not?*
- Learners look at the example. Ask *Why has 'late', but not 'early', got a circle around it?* (late is the correct word) Learners complete the task in pairs. They can check their answers in the story. Ask different pairs to read out one of the complete correct sentences in open class.
- Practise the difference in pronunciation between *angry* and *hungry*. Ask two or three learners to mime either *I'm angry* or *I'm hungry*. Other learners guess what they are feeling by saying *You are angry!* or *You are hungry!*

Answers

2 loved **3** glue **4** dictionary **5** map **6** angry

Extension

In pairs, learners choose three sentences and extend them with *because* or *to* for purpose. They write these in their notebooks and then read them out in open class. Learners can look in the story for *because* and *to* clauses to help them.
Suggestions:
2 The children in William's class loved his stories <u>because they were funny.</u>
3 William took some glue to school with him that day <u>to stick some pictures in his book.</u>
4 The alien ate William's English dictionary <u>because it looked like food.</u>

 C **Who's talking about this story? Listen and tick the correct box.**

- Learners look at the pictures. Say *These three friends have just read different stories. Only one of them is talking about 'William's strangest story'. Was it David, Betty or Frank? Listen.*
- **19** Play the audio twice if necessary. Ask *Was it David? Was it Betty? Was it Frank?* Learners put up their hands to show which answer they think is right.
- Ask *Why isn't the answer David or Frank?* (David – William didn't go to another planet. Frank – William didn't meet the alien in a strange dream.)

Answer

Betty

Tapescript:
David
David: Hi. My name's David. I've just read a story about a boy who travels to another planet where he meets a huge alien. He gets really worried about that because it's dangerous! But the boy is safe at the end of the story because he comes back to Earth.

Betty
Betty: Hello. I'm Betty. The story that I've just read is about a boy in a spaceship. It's quite scary, but the boy isn't frightened or worried about anything. I think he's brave and funny. An alien wants to find out about the things in his backpack!

Frank
Frank: I'm Frank. Hi! This story is about a boy who has strange dreams. He dreams he's going to be late for school. But the boy is lazy and says 'I don't mind' in his dream. Then he meets an alien who takes him to school in a spaceship! That part was funny.

D Choose the best answer. Write a letter (A–G).

- Say *William is talking to his classmate, Oliver.* Learners look at the example.
- Ask two learners to read out the question and the answer marked *B*. Say *Oliver asked a question. William answered it.* Learners could cross out *B* from William's possible answers.
- Say *Now you match the answers to the questions. Write the letter. There are two answers in A to G that you don't need.* Learners complete the conversation, writing just the letter on the dotted line. Check answers in open class, asking two or three pairs to read out each exchange in full.

Answers
2 D   3 G   4 A   5 F

- Say *Show me an angry face! Now look worried/bored/happy!* Learners pull faces.
- Ask *Which problems did William have in the story?* (he was late, he fell over, he woke up on a spaceship, he cut up the alien's space map) *Did he get angry? Frightened?* (no) *What does he say in Activity D when his friend, Oliver, broke his pen?* (That's OK. Never mind!)
- In L1 if necessary, ask learners again about the message of this story. Divide learners into groups of three or four. Say *If you want to, talk about the last time you were worried or angry.* Walk around and help with vocabulary if necessary.
- Learners continue working in their groups. Each group talks about one of the following scenarios. Say *Don't worry or get angry! What can you do?*
  - *You can't play in tomorrow's volleyball match because you've hurt your knee.*
  - *It begins to rain while you are walking home from school and you don't have a rain coat.*
  - *You forgot to take some water with you on a long walk.*
  - *Your favourite programme will start in five minutes, but the TV isn't working.*

E William is talking to Mrs Lake about school. What must he take to each lesson? Listen and write a letter in each box.

- With books closed, ask *What subjects do children learn at school?* (YLE word list: geography, music, science, history, maths, English, languages, art, gym)
- Note that school subjects are often written with a capital letter, but can also be written with a lower-case first letter. Learners can use either in the Flyers test.
- Ask *Which four things did William have to take to school in the story?* (a dictionary, scissors, glue and wool) *Which subjects did he need them for?* (English, art, history and geography)
- Learners open their books and look at the six school subjects and the example. Say *Listen to William and his teacher, Mrs Lake. She's telling William to bring different things to his next six lessons. What must William take to his English lesson?* (a key)

20

- Play the audio twice. Learners listen and write a letter in each box.
- Check answers. Ask *Which things doesn't William need?* (the football, the spoon)

Answers
science B   maths E   music A   geography G   history F

Tapescript:

Listen and look. There is one example.

Boy:	What do we have to bring to school tomorrow, Mrs Lake? I've forgotten.
Woman:	Well, your first lesson will be English, William. Please bring a small metal key to that one.
Boy:	The one that starts the engine in my dad's car?
Woman:	No, William. Not that one!

Can you see the letter D? Now you listen and write a letter in each box.

Boy:	We'll have a science class tomorrow too.
Woman:	That's right. I hope you like drawing. You're going to need a leaf in that lesson.
Boy:	Why?
Woman:	You'll have to draw it and then learn about watering and feeding different plants.
Boy:	Oh!
Woman:	You'll have history after the break.
Boy:	Great.
Woman:	Have you got something with an old stamp on it at home?
Boy:	Mmm, I'm not sure. We might have.
Woman:	Well, bring it if you can find one. If you can't find one, don't worry. I can give you something in the lesson.
Boy:	What else will we study tomorrow?
Woman:	Geography. I might teach that class, but I'm not sure about that yet.
Boy:	OK. What do I need to bring for that? A ruler again? I hope not. I've broken mine.
Woman:	Never mind. You just need some salt.
Boy:	Why?
Woman:	You'll find out tomorrow. It'll be fun.
Boy:	Have we got maths after lunch as well?
Woman:	Yes. Please don't bring your football into class again like you did last week.
Boy:	All right!
Woman:	But you will need a ruler in that lesson. Is that going to be a problem?
Boy:	No. I can borrow Oliver's. It's a plastic one, but it'll be all right.

Woman:	Your last lesson will be music. I'm going to show you something interesting in that class.
Boy:	What? Will we use spoons again to make those funny sounds?
Woman:	Not this time. Please bring a comb with you to that lesson.
Boy:	OK. I've only got an old one.
Woman:	That's all right. But please wash it before you put it in your school bag!

Test tip: FLYERS
Listening (Part 3)

✔ Learners hear a conversation and have to match pictures from two different sets. There is one example, then five pictures in the first set, e.g. different relatives, possessions or jobs, and seven pictures in the second set.

Learners write *A–H* to show the match in tick boxes in the first set. The first set is not heard in the order shown.

→ Get learners used to quickly spotting where to write their *A–H* answers. Learners draw in their notebooks five or six Flyers possessions, e.g. a key, a flag, a backpack, some scissors, a drum, a torch, in a vertical column, adding tick boxes. Learners use a pencil to write *A–H*. Say in random order, e.g. *Where's the torch? Write C there. Where's the flag? Write A there.*

Learners could then erase their answers so you could repeat the task with different answers.

F Answer the alien. Look and say.

- Learners read again *William showed it his pair of scissors ... 'For cutting,' William said* on page 46. Write on the board: *We use this for ...-ing.*

- Learners look at Activity F. Ask *What is in these pictures?* (a knife, some money, some soap, a phone, a hair dryer, a key) Say *Look! The alien asks 'What are these for?' Can you answer its question?*

- Review/Teach *hair dryer*. Write it on the board, underlining *hair* and *dry*. Then ask *What is the knife for?* Accept any valid answer, e.g. *We use this for cutting food / putting butter on bread / opening envelopes.*

- Review/Teach words to describe different materials. Write *It's made of ...* on the board. Ask different learners for words to complete the sentence and add those to the board, e.g. *card, glass, plastic, metal, wood, paper, wool, silver, gold.* Check understanding by pointing to different objects in the classroom and asking *What's this book/chair/ring/window/desk made of?*

- In small groups, learners write answers for each picture. Different learners read out a sentence. Other groups guess the object, e.g. *It's for washing your hands. Soap!*

- Pairs can role play their dialogues. Learners take turns to ask a question and give an answer for another household/classroom object.

Extension

Write on the board:
This is / These are made of _____. We use it/them for _____ .
Divide learners into A pairs and B pairs. Give each A pair the A set and each B pair the B set of nine pictures from Photocopy 6B (TB page 60), cut into cards. Pairs look at their pictures and whisper together to make two sentences to describe each object without naming it, using the model on the board, e.g. *These are made of metal. We use them for cutting.* (scissors)
One A pair and one B pair work together. Pairs take turns to describe one of their picture cards without showing or naming it. The other pair guesses it as quickly as possible. When the right answer is guessed, the pair who described it puts their picture card face up on the table. Learners play the game for about five minutes or until they tire of the game. The pair with the most picture cards face up on the table are the winners.

G Read the story. Choose a word from the box. Write the correct words next to numbers 1–5.

- Learners look at the example. Ask *Where are the missing words?* (in the word box) *How many gaps are there?* (five) *How many other words in the box can you use for your answers?* (nine) Say *You don't need to use all the words.*

- Learners work on their own to complete the text and choose the best name for the story. Check answers by asking learners to take turns to read out a sentence. Learners vote for the best answer.

- Say *The alien tasted some of Oliver's crayons. Which colour tasted horrible?* (blue) *And delicious?* (red) *What does the alien decide to eat instead?* (a burger) *Who believed Oliver's story?* (his best friend)

Answers

1 astronaut **2** happened **3** speak **4** gates **5** broken
6 Oliver's unusual morning

Test tip: FLYERS
Reading and Writing (Part 3)

✔ Learners choose the correct title for a story from a choice of three. Before learners complete the text with the five missing words and choose the title, encourage them to read the whole text to get a general understanding of the story.

→ Ask learners to choose one right and one wrong title for short texts, poems or songs. Ask why one is right and the other is wrong. You might also ask learners to think of good alternative titles for all the stories in the book. Ask questions like *Who's the most important person in this story?* to help learners develop this skill.

H Find the words that sound the same. Draw lines.

- Say *Some words look different but sound the same.* Write on the board: *right, wood* and *their.* Ask *Do you know other words that have different spellings, but sound the same as these? Can you find them in the story?* (write, would and there) Write the answers on the board to show the three same-sounding pairs.

- Learners look at the two sets of words. Say *Now find words that have different spellings but only sound the same at the end.* Ask *Which word sounds like 'bed'?* (said) In pairs, learners draw lines to words with the same end sound. Encourage pairs to check by saying the words out loud.
- Check answers in open class.

Answers

see/key glue/threw late/eight use/choose
full/wool some/mum my/Hi! floor/sure
knees/please

I   Look at the pictures. Find six differences.

- Learners look at the pictures. Ask *Where's William?* (inside the spaceship) Say *Some things in these pictures are the same and some are different.*
- Point to the first picture and say *William's holding some …* (scissors) Point to the second picture and say *But in this picture, he's holding a …* (torch)
- Write on the board: *In this picture* _____ *, but in this picture* _____ *.*
- In groups of three or four, learners find six other differences and think how to describe them. Different groups explain one difference.

Answers

In this picture there's a planet with a ring in the window, but in this picture there isn't a planet with a ring.
In this picture the wool is in the bag, but in this picture the wool is on the floor.
In this picture the map is in William's hands, but in this picture the map is next to his feet.
In this picture the screen is on, but in this picture the screen is off.
In this picture the alien has got 10 teeth, but in this picture the alien has got 11 teeth.
In this picture the pipes are moving, but in this picture the pipes aren't moving.

Extension

Learners write three sentences about any of the other pictures in the story. Learners read out their sentences. Other learners listen and say which picture they are describing.

J   Why were you late today? Complete your funny story.

- Ask *Can you remember any of William's strange stories? The ones he told his teacher when he was late for school? What did he say?* Learners could look on page 44. (Our dog ate my maths homework. My little sister threw my school uniform in the bath. Someone drove away Dad's car at midnight last night, so I had to walk all the way here.)
- Say *Now you think of some strange or funny stories about being late.* In groups of three or four, learners think of three reasons why they arrived at school late today. Brainstorm ideas in open class before the group work if necessary, e.g. *I had to help our pet monkey climb down a tree. An eagle used all my socks to make a nest.* Encourage learners to be creative.
- Learners complete the story. Walk around and help with vocabulary if necessary. Ask different learners to read out their stories.

Let's have fun!

Read the information. Make a planet mobile.

Learners look at page 70, Activity 6. They use the information about the size of the planets to make a planet mobile. First they draw and cut out planets from card. Then they could paint them and attach different lengths of string or wool to each one and hang them on a coat hanger or circular ring of wire. Display the mobiles in the classroom if possible.

Let's speak!

Ask and answer about travelling.

Learners look at page 73, Activity 6. Ask the class *How do people travel round our town?* (learners answer) Then ask different learners *Have you ever been on a ship?* and *How do you travel round your town?* Learners then take turns to ask and answer these two questions in pairs. When they have finished talking, ask four or five learners *How do you travel round your town?* You could write *by bus, by car, I cycle, I walk,* etc. on the board. Point to each way to travel. Learners put up their hands if this is the way they travel. Then ask *How do most students in this class travel round town?*

33

 Let's say!

Say *Look at page 75, Activity 6. Listen.* Play the audio. Ask *Did you hear the /əʊ/ sounds in go, home, yellow, phone, coat, show, stone?*
Say each word. Learners repeat in chorus. They could circle the /əʊ/ sounds on the page.
Learners listen to the rhyme again.
Say *Let's say this again. Quickly or slowly!* Learners repeat the rhyme in chorus.
Say *There's an /əʊ/ sound in 'slowly' too. Can you hear it? Can you think of more story words with the sound /əʊ/ in them?* Learners find words in the story. Write their suggestions on the board. (e.g. those, homework, so, Oh!, opened, OK, going, elbows, broken)
You could also show learners that *know/no* and *rode/road* sound exactly the same.

Home FUN booklet

➡ **Pages 20–21 school**
➡ **Picture dictionary: school**

Go online

to practise your English
to listen to the audio recordings
to find more FUN activities!

7 The past and the future

Main topics:	transport, IT, home
Story summary:	Helen and Robert explore the top rooms of their house. A boy from the future steps out of a broken mirror and tells them about everything which is different.
Main grammar:	*still, ago, will* (prediction), *could* (hypothetical), *should, by myself/yourself,* tenses review
Main vocabulary:	*ambulance, astronauts, broken into pieces, century, dark, earth, information, invitation, letter, passenger, puzzle, rockets, skyscrapers, taxi*
Value:	Being inspired by people (*"Let me try!"*)
Let's say!:	/aɪ/
Practice tasks:	Reading and Writing Part 4 (D), Listening Part 4 (E), Reading and Writing Part 3 (H)
Test tasks:	Speaking Part 1 (F), Reading and Writing Part 6 (G)

Equipment:	audio: Storytelling, C, E, I, Let's say!	• blank stickers: A Extension

➔ (presentation **PLUS**) flashcards

Go to Presentation plus to find pictures of Flyers vocabulary from Unit 7. You can use the pictures to teach/review important words in this unit.

➔ (presentation **PLUS**) Image carousel 38–44

(invitation, space, astronaut, rocket, skyscraper, puzzle, taxi): Storytelling

• Photocopy 7, one per learner (TB page 61): Let's have fun!
• crayons or colouring pencils: Let's have fun!

Storytelling

Before listening

With books closed …

*   Introduce the topic of the story. Ask *Would you like to live 150 years in the past? Why? / Why not? What can we do now that we couldn't do then?* (learners answer) Say *This story is about a brother and a sister who lived 150 years ago. They meet and then talk to someone who lives in our time now!*

*   Use the Image carousel to review/teach *invitation, space, astronaut, rocket, skyscraper.* Ask *What might you read about in an invitation?* (a birthday party) *Who travels through space in rockets?* (astronauts) *Where do you see skyscrapers?* (in big cities) Review/Teach *century.* Ask *What year is it now?* (e.g. 2017) Say *This year begins with '20' but, actually, we live in the 21st century.* Remember you can use the flashcards on Presentation plus to help you teach and review vocabulary.

*   Look at the first story picture without the story text on the Image carousel or with the story text in the book on page 52. Ask *Is this a large or small house?* (large) *Where is it?* (learners guess – in London) *What time of year is it?* (autumn) *Someone is looking out of a window. Who is that?* (learners guess – the girl in the story) *Do you think this is the past, the present or the future?* (learners guess – the past)

*   Say *Now let's listen to the story.* Say *Let's look at page 52.*

Listening

With books open …

Play the audio or read the story. Learners listen.

Play the audio or read the story again.

21
*   Pause after *He was trying to say something but his words, like the glass in the mirror, were broken into small pieces* on page 53. Ask *What were the brother and sister's names?* (Robert and Helen) *What did they find in this room?* (a broken mirror, a bookcase, a violin, a chess set, a skateboard, a phone) *Which three things were in the bookcase?* (a spider and two pieces of paper) *Who appeared when Helen read the message?* (the boy in the mirror) *What do you think will happen next?* (learners guess)

*   Pause after *'It's called a phone,' the boy said. 'I came back for that too.'* on page 54. Ask *Did the boy visit Robert and Helen from their past or their future?* (their future) *Which two things did the boy want to collect from the room?* (his skateboard and his phone) *What did the boy say people can do on a computer?* (watch moving pictures, listen to and read information, do puzzles, draw cartoons, play learning games) *Who helped Helen to skateboard across the room?* (Robert) *What was Helen holding?* (a phone)

After listening

- After listening to the whole story, say *The boy told Helen and Robert about cars, ambulances, buses, taxis, skyscrapers and …* (airports, planes, astronauts, rockets) *Who did Robert want to meet after the boy left?* (someone from the past) *Why did Helen need a pencil?* (learners guess – to draw a flying machine)

 Value

- In L1, discuss what can happen when we feel inspired by other people. Ask *Do you think Helen or Robert was most inspired by the boy's information about the future?* (Helen) *What does Helen say in the story that shows she's inspired by what she hears?* ('Let me try!' 'What else is different in the future?' 'Flying machines? Where's my favourite drawing pencil?') *Who inspires you to try harder or do something new? Have you ever seen a film or read a story that has inspired you in some way? Perhaps to want to explore the world or study, when you are older, to do a special kind of job?* Accept answers in English or L1.

Extension

Ask *If you could choose to travel to any part of the world, back or forward in time, where would you go and to which century? Why?* In groups of three or four, learners discuss this and come to a group decision. They then complete a sentence to report back to the class:
Our group would like to travel to _____
in the _____ century because we'd like to
_____ .

 A **Put the travelling words on the suitcase and things you write or draw on the screen.**

- Learners look at the coloured words. Ask *What's the first word?* (taxi) *Do you travel in a taxi or is it something you write?* (you travel in a taxi) *Which word is under 'taxi'?* (letter) *Do you travel in a letter or write it?* (write it)
- Point to the drawings and ask *What are these?* (a suitcase, a computer screen) Say *Write the things about travel on the suitcase. Write the things you can write or draw on the computer screen.*
- Learners compare their answers in pairs and then check in open class.

Answers

suitcase: ambulance, wheels, passenger, space
computer: puzzle, invitation, letter, cartoon, information

Extension

Adding articles (*a/an/the*), write words from Activity A and/or other nouns from the story onto blank stickers. Make enough for one per learner. Stick a vocabulary sticker on each learner's back. Learners should not see the word. Learners walk around and ask *yes/no* questions to find out what their word is. Model this by showing learners a sticker. Say *Mine says 'a phone'.* Stick it on your own back. Ask *Am I small?* (yes) *Can you travel in me?* (no) *Am I made of paper?* (no) *Can you carry me?* (yes) *Have I got numbers on me?* (yes) *Do you use me to talk to friends?* (yes) *Am I a phone?* (yes)
You could write all the possible answers on the board and the following question starters: *Am I …? Can I …? Have I got …? Am I made of …? Do you use me for/to …?*

 B **Read and tick the correct box.**

- Ask *What do we know about Helen?* (e.g. She lived in London about 150 years ago. Her brother was called Robert.) *What don't we know about her?* (her age / family name / favourite colour, food, hobbies, etc.)

- Learners look at Activity B. Ask *Is the first sentence about the story right, wrong, or must we say 'don't know'?* (right) *And the second sentence? We …* (don't know) *Now you read and tick the correct box. If you can't remember, find the answers in the story.*
- Check answers in open class.

Answers

3 wrong   **4** wrong   **5** don't know   **6** right   **7** right
8 don't know

 C **Look, read and draw lines. Then listen and check.**

- Ask *Do you know who invented each of these things?* Learners discuss in pairs and look online if possible. Learners draw lines between the pictures and the names.
- Play the audio. Learners listen and check.

22

- Check answers in open class. Point to *Alexander Graham Bell* and say *This person invented something that we use every day. People couldn't carry the first ones in their pockets, but they can now. What is it?* (the telephone) Point to *Karl Drais* and say *This person invented something which millions of people have now. They use their feet to make it move. What is it?* (a bicycle) Say *And we think Konrad Zuse invented the first …* (computer)

Tapescript:

Woman: We think Karl Von Drais invented the bicycle in 1817.

  Some people say that Konrad Zuse invented the first computer in 1936.

  A man called Alexander Graham Bell invented the telephone in 1876, we think.

- In L1 if necessary, ask learners again about the message of the story. Accept all valid answers.
- In L1, ask *What do you think inspired these three people to invent these inventions?* (e.g. Need? Fame? Wealth? Ambition? Wanting to help their community? An interest in engineering?)
- Ask *What do you think Helen will be when she's an adult? And Robert?* Learners guess their jobs. Ask *Who or what are you most inspired by? Famous sportsmen and women? Pop stars? Inventors? Artists? Teachers? Parents? Friends?*

- Ask *Have you got any ideas about something you would like to invent? What makes you want to do that?* Divide learners into groups of three or four. Learners talk about things they would like to invent and why. Walk around and help with vocabulary if necessary. Ask different groups to tell the class their ideas in English or L1.

Read and circle the correct answer.

- Learners look at the example. Ask *Why is there a circle around 'be'?* (it's the correct answer)
- Learners work in pairs or on their own to choose and circle the right answers.
- Check answers by asking different learners to read out one of the sentences.
- Ask *How many people in this class watch TV on computers or tablets now? How much time do you spend playing video games? Do you think people will live on the moon in the future?*

Answers						
2 by	**3** In	**4** few	**5** playing	**6** could	**7** doing	

Listen and tick the box.

23

- Learners look at the questions and picture answers. Say *You're going to listen to Harry, Clare and their parents. Read the questions carefully and tick the right box.*
- Play the audio twice. Learners work on their own and tick box A, B or C for each answer.
- Check answers in open class. After choosing the right picture answer, ask a different learner to answer each question using a complete sentence, e.g. *Which job does Harry want to do one day?* (He wants to be a famous artist.)

Answers			
1 B	**2** C	**3** B	**4** A

Tapescript:

1 Which job does Harry want to do one day?

Woman:	What do you want to be one day, Harry? An actor?
Boy:	And work in a theatre? No, thanks. I'd like to be a famous artist, actually.
Woman:	Really?
Boy:	Yes, I don't think I want to be a teacher. That's too difficult.

2 What is Clare reading about now?

Girl:	Good morning, Father.
Man:	Hello, Clare. Is that another book about machines?
Girl:	No, different types of medicine. I'm very interested in learning more about that.
Man:	Well, that's good, but have you done your violin practice today?
Girl:	No, but I will later.
Man:	Excellent.

3 When will the family go on holiday?

Girl:	Can we still go on holiday this winter, Mother?
Woman:	I'm sorry, not this year, but we will have a holiday next year.
Girl:	In the spring?
Woman:	That will be too soon. In the autumn. That's a nice time of year for a holiday, I think.

4 Where is the chess set?

Girl:	Have you seen my chess set?
Boy:	Isn't it on that old seat? It was there yesterday.
Girl:	I know. But it's not there now, and it isn't on the shelf where we usually put it.
Boy:	Well, have you looked on the swing?
Girl:	No, I haven't. But … oh, you're right! That's where it is. Great!

Look at the pictures. Talk about six differences.

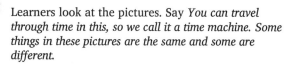

- Learners look at the pictures. Say *You can travel through time in this, so we call it a time machine. Some things in these pictures are the same and some are different.*
- Point to the first picture and say *The roofs in this picture are …* (red) Point to the second picture and say *But in this picture, they're …* (brown)
- Write on the board:
  In this picture _____ , but in this picture _____ .
- In pairs, learners look at the two pictures and talk about the differences. They use the sentence on the board to help them.
- Check answers in open class. Learners only need to describe six differences, but there are 12 differences in total here. Ask *Has anyone found more than ten / all 12 differences?*

Answers
In this picture there's a picture of an eagle on the side of the machine, but in this picture there's a picture of a penguin.
In this picture the mirror is broken, but in this picture the mirror is not broken.
In this picture there are three wheels, but in this picture there are two wheels.
In this picture the chessboard is in front of the violin, but in this picture the chessboard is behind the violin.
In this picture the boy is wearing a cap, but in this picture he is wearing a helmet.
In this picture it is two o'clock, but in this picture it is five o'clock.
In this picture the boy is wearing a scarf, but in this picture he isn't wearing a scarf.
In this picture there isn't a person behind the skyscraper window, but in this picture there is a person behind the window.
In this picture the stripes on the rocket are yellow, but in this picture the stripes are blue.
In this picture the boy looks worried, but in this picture he looks happy.
In this picture there are three stars on the front of the machine, but in this picture there are three planets.

✔ Learners have to spot and explain five of several visible differences between two pictures. These may relate to, e.g. colour, number, size, position, activity, time and absence or presence of something/someone.

→ Use any picture to practise identifying these details. Ask *What colour …?, Which is bigger/smaller …?, Where …?, What … doing …?, When …?, What does it look like …?* questions.

Extension

Say *You are a journalist. You find out that someone has seen a time machine. Write about this for your online newspaper.* Learners choose one of the pictures and describe what is happening in their notebooks.

G Read the diary and write the missing words. Write one word on each line.

- Learners read the first two sentences. Ask *Where did this person go today?* (to a special museum) Ask *Was this a school trip or a place a family visited on holiday?* (a school trip) Ask *What do people learn about in museums?* (e.g. their history, famous people, old clothes, old ways of travelling, animals, paintings)

- Say *Some words are missing. Can you see the missing words?* (no) Make sure learners understand that they must read carefully and choose one word that will fit in each space.

- Learners complete the text on their own.

- Ask *Would you like to be a designer one day? What kind of things would you like to design?*

Suggested answers

1 wore   **2** there   **3** sit/read   **4** was   **5** That/It

✔ Learners should only use one word to complete the gaps in the diary/message/letter text. Make sure learners understand that only one word will be necessary in a correct answer. The missing word may come from part of a common phrase, e.g. *to take a photo*.

→ Try to teach new verbs and nouns within meaningful phrases, e.g. *to **borrow** a ruler or pen, to **whisper** a secret to a friend, to **save** a file on the computer, an **actor** might work in a theatre, to carry things in a **backpack** on your back, to clean your teeth with a toothbrush and **toothpaste**.*

H Read and write a word from the box.

- Ask *Would you like to live in the past like Helen and Robert? Why? / Why not?* (learners answer)

- Learners look at Activity H. Say *Here's some more information about the future for Helen and Robert.* Tell learners to cover the words in the box with a piece of paper or their hand. Ask different learners to read out a sentence. The class guesses the words for each space. Learners do not write anything yet.

- Say *Now read the text again, and choose the correct word from the box.* Learners complete the text. Check answers in open class by asking questions, e.g. *What can students do on computers?* (look for information) *What does the most boring, difficult or dangerous jobs?* (robots / men that are made of plastic and metal)

Answers

2 look   **3** metal   **4** buildings   **5** wonderful   **6** move

I Listen and write the words.

- Say *This poem is about learning different things at school and at home.* Ask different learners *What do you enjoy learning about most?* (learners answer)

- Ask *Can you guess the missing words?* In L1 if necessary, point out that the words at the ends of the lines rhyme, e.g. *caves/brave, snow/grow,* so the missing words will rhyme with *stones, night, pockets* and *stop.* In pairs, learners read the poem and try to guess the four missing words.

- Say *Now let's listen and write.*

- Play the audio. Learners listen and check their answers.

24

Answers

1 phones   **2** light   **3** rockets   **4** top

Tapescript:

See SB and Answers

Extension

Divide the class into small groups. Learners try to complete another verse for the poem about the things they enjoy learning about. Tell them not to worry about making their words rhyme.
Write on the board:
I'm learning about _____
and _____ .
I'm learning about _____
What a _____ !
I'm learning about _____
Oh! And how to _____ .
Groups read out their verse in open class.

7 Let's have fun!

Design your own time machine.

Learners look at page 71, Activity 7. In pairs or small groups, they read the questions and talk about their ideas. Give each learner Photocopy 7 (TB page 61). They draw their time machine designs and write a description below. When they have finished, learners could show their time machines and talk about them to the class. Display learners' time machines on the classroom wall if possible.

7 Let's speak!

What will you do/be? Ask and answer to find out.

Learners look at page 73, Activity 7. You could brainstorm jobs that learners find exciting or interesting and also review/teach all the different jobs on the YLE word list:

Starters and Movers: *clown, cook, dentist, doctor, driver, farmer, film star, nurse, pirate, pop star, teacher*

Flyers: *actor, artist, astronaut, businessman/woman, designer, engineer, fire fighter, journalist, manager, mechanic, photographer, pilot, police officer, queen, singer, waiter*

Learners walk around and take turns to ask and answer different classmates about their future jobs.

Ask several learners what they would like to be and then ask *What do quite a lot of students in this class want to be?*

Learners could then make an origami 'fortune teller'. See www.youtube.com/watch?v = y4SnzwjriGg for a video online.

Give each learner a piece of paper that is about 150 cm square. Give instructions to learners in L1:

1 Fold the paper in half along one of the diagonals. Unfold it again. Fold the paper again along the other diagonal. Unfold it again.

2 Fold all four corners into the centre.

3 Turn the paper over so it is a smaller flat square shape. Write eight jobs in the eight sections of the square.

4 Fold the corners to meet in the centre again. Write numbers 1–8 in the eight sections.

5 Turn the paper over again and write four colours (one in each corner).

6 Fold the fortune teller in half. Open the fortune teller so you can get a finger and thumb in each side. Open and close the fortune teller in two different ways.

Learners then work in pairs, taking turns to choose a colour (their partner spelling out the colour as they open and close the fortune teller) and then a number (their partner counting up to the number as they open and close the fortune teller) to reveal their future job.

Ask different learners *Is your job the same as the one you talked about before?*

34

( ) **Let's say!**

Say *Look at page 75, Activity 7. Listen.* Play the audio. Ask *Did you hear the /aɪ/ sounds in I, designed, time, science, tried, fly, high, sky?*
Say each word. Learners repeat in chorus. They could circle the /aɪ/ sounds on the page.
Learners listen to the rhyme again.
Say *Would you like to say this too?* Learners repeat the rhyme in chorus.
Say *There's an /aɪ/ sound in 'like' too. Can you hear it? Can you think of more story words with the sound /aɪ/ in them?* Learners find words in the story. Write their suggestions on the board. (e.g. find, right, lights, violin, spider, writing, Hi!, surprised, ride, mine, bicycles, drive, skyscrapers)
You could also show learners that *I/eye* and *right/write* sound exactly the same.

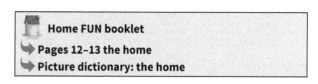

Home FUN booklet

➡ **Pages 12–13 the home**
➡ **Picture dictionary: the home**

Go online

to practise your English
to listen to the audio recordings
to find more FUN activities!

The School of Science

8

Main topics:	school, work, jobs
Story summary:	Sarah and Sam study unusual things at the School of Science.
Main grammar:	*still, will, going to*, present continuous, prepositions of time
Main vocabulary:	*biscuit, brush, dark, dates, delicious, designer, diary, engineer, fetch, fire, gloves, hour, ice, journalist, left, mechanic, medicine, midnight, pepper, pilot, program, pull off, remember, right, robot, salt, screen, term, through, timetable, toe, unusual, X-ray*
Value:	Being curious (*"It's so interesting!"*)
Let's say!:	/ə/
Practice tasks:	Reading and Writing Part 1 (A), Reading and Writing Part 5 (B), Reading and Writing Part 4 (D), Listening Part 3 (G), Speaking Part 3 (H)
Test tasks:	Listening Part 4 (E), Reading and Writing Part 7 (H)
Equipment:	• audio: Storytelling, E, G, Let's say! • ▸ (presentation **PLUS**) flashcards Go to Presentation plus to find pictures of Flyers vocabulary from Unit 8. You can use the pictures to teach/review important words in this unit. • ▸ (presentation **PLUS**) Image carousel 45–55 (engineer, journalist, restaurant manager, mechanic, pilot; fingers, toes, bones; astronaut, designer, twins): Storytelling • shoe box for each pair of learners, paper, glue, crayons, colouring pencils or paint: Let's have fun!

 Storytelling

Before listening

With books closed …

- Introduce the topic of the story. Say *Some people think that science is one of the most important school subjects. What do you think? Do you enjoy finding out about things that people have invented? This story is about a brother and sister called Sam and Sarah. Sam and Sarah go to a really funny school called 'The School of Science'. They have lots of fun there.*

- Review/Teach *engineer, journalist, restaurant manager, mechanic* and *pilot* using the pictures on the Image carousel. Ask *Who might design a bridge / work for a newspaper / give instructions to waiters and cooks / repair a car engine / fly a plane?* (an engineer, a journalist, a restaurant manager, a mechanic, a pilot) Use the Image carousel to review/teach *fingers, toes* and *bones*. Say *Show me your fingers! Point to your toes! Did you know that you have 27 bones in each hand?* Review/Teach *left* and *right*. Say *Touch your left ear / right elbow. Hold up your right/left hand.* Remember you can use the flashcards on Presentation plus to help you teach and review vocabulary.

- Look at the first story picture without the story text on the Image carousel or with the story text in the book on page 60. Say *This is Sarah and Sam. They are twins, so they are the same age. Do you know any twins? Do they look the same or different?* Learners look at the second picture. Review/Teach *X-ray* (you could use the photograph of *bones* on the Image carousel). Say *One of the teachers has invented this machine. Does this look like the kind of science lesson that students usually have? Why? / Why not?*

- Say *Now let's listen to the story.* Say *Let's look at page 60.*

Listening

With books open …

▶ Play the audio or read the story. Learners listen.

25 Play the audio or read the story again.

- Pause after *'Well, don't worry! You'll be OK again by dinner time'* on page 61. Ask *Where do the students have to put their hands in their first lesson?* (inside the special X-ray machine) *What colour are Sarah's bones now?* (blue) *What did the students use to make the special chocolate in Mrs Pool's class?* (coffee beans, milk, pepper and lime juice) *What date does Sam remember when he tastes the chocolate?* (June 11th) *Who gave him a strawberry milkshake that day?* (his grandmother)

- Pause after *'Don't worry! You'll be dry again by midnight.'* at the end of page 62. Ask *What mustn't the children drop in Mr Spot's class?* (the glue) *What changed the ice to water in Mrs Wetter's class?* (the special salt) *Who got very wet?* (Sam)

After listening

- After listening to the whole story, ask *What might the twins write for the school robot the next day?* (a computer program) *And what was for dinner?* (carrot biscuits, fish milkshakes, meatball and tomato sauce sandwiches) *Do you think that meal will be delicious?* (learners guess) *Who else went to The School of Science?* (the twins' mother) *Would you like to study there too? Why? / Why not?*

 Value

- In L1 if necessary, discuss the importance of being curious about the world we live in. Ask *How does building your knowledge by learning lots of different things help you in your future life? How useful is the internet? How do you learn best – with or without a teacher?* Ask *Can you remember any times when you've been really curious about something and wanted to find out more about it?* (learners answer) *What's the most interesting, most surprising or strangest thing you've ever learned?* Put learners' ideas on the board. The class votes for the strangest or most interesting fact. Accept answers in English or L1.

 A · **Read and write a job from the box.**

- With books closed, play a word association game. Explain, in L1 if necessary, that you are going to say a job and then learners say the first word they think of, e.g. *Cook!* Different learners: *plates, food, oven, restaurant, café, delicious!* Continue to play with more jobs that learners know, e.g. *actor, artist, astronaut, clown, dentist, designer, doctor, engineer, farmer, film star, fire fighter, photographer, police officer, pop star.*

- With books open, learners look at the example and at the words in the box and circles. Ask *When you read the words in each circle, which job do you think of?* Learners work on their own and write the jobs on the lines.

Answers

2 a journalist   **3** a mechanic   **4** an astronaut
5 a designer   **6** a pilot

 B · **Complete the sentences. Write 1, 2 or 3 words.**

- Learners look at the example sentence. Ask *How many words can you write to complete each sentence?* (one, two or three)

- Learners work in pairs to decide how to complete sentences 2–6. Ask different pairs to read out one finished sentence. Their classmates put up their hands if they agree.

Answers

2 Sam / Sarah's brother   **3** some (amazing) glue
4 bridges   **5** (new)(school) robot   **6** School of Science

Extension

The students write a program for the new school robot. Learners imagine they are going to do this. In pairs, they write ten things that they want the school robot to be able to do. They could begin their list with *We are going to program the robot so it can:*
Pairs work with other pairs and choose ten things (of their 20) that they want the robot to do. They feed back in open class.

 C · **Write your dream school timetable. Choose your own subjects or use ideas from the box.**

- Learners read the subjects in the box. Check understanding of *IT* (information technology). Ask *Which school subject is the easiest / the most interesting/ exciting/important? Are all your favourite subjects here? What other subjects would you like to study?* (e.g. drama, astronomy, photography, medicine, dancing)

- Learners look at Activity C. Ask *What's this?* (a timetable) Check understanding of *am* and *pm* Ask *Which means a time after midnight, in the morning and before midday?* (am) *Which means a time after midday, in the afternoon and evening and before midnight?* (pm)

- Say *Choose and write your dream school timetable.* Explain that *dream* here means *perfect.* Learners talk about the timetable in pairs and then work on their own to complete it. They can include the subjects in the word box and any others they would like to study.

- Learners talk about their dream timetable in small groups and then in open class.

- In L1 if necessary, ask learners again about the message of this story. Ask *If you did have this dream timetable at school, which subject would you be most curious about? What would you want to learn more about most of all?* Learners discuss these questions in groups. Walk around and help with vocabulary if necessary. Ask different groups to tell the class their answers in English or L1.

 D · **Complete the sentences with** *by, until, for, ago, during* **or** *while*.

- Review/Teach time prepositions *for, since, ago* and *during.*

- Review/Teach *by, until* and *while.* Ask learners to find and underline the following sentences in the story:

  'Your fingers will be OK again <u>by</u> tea time.' (page 60)

  'But you can't eat it <u>until</u> next week.' (page 61)

  'Don't touch anything <u>while</u> I go and get a towel.' (page 62)

- Ask *Who said each thing?* (Mr Basket, Mrs Pool and Mrs Wetter)

- Ask *Will Sarah's fingers be OK before tea time?* (yes) Explain that *by* means *no later than* here. Ask *Can the students eat the chocolate this week?* (no) Explain that *until* means *not before* here. Ask *Can the students touch the ice and salt when Mrs Wetter is out of the room?* (no) *Can they touch the ice and salt when Mrs Wetter is back in the classroom?* (yes) Explain that *while* is used to talk about two things that happen at the same time.
- To help show the meanings of *by*, *while* and *until*, write on the board '*I will be home again by five o'clock, Mum. Can you wash my football shorts while I am out? I don't need them until Saturday, but they're really dirty!*' Learners repeat the sentences in chorus.
- Learners look at the example in Activity D. Say *Use the words to complete the sentences.* Learners work on their own or in pairs. Check answers in open class.

Answers

2 for　**3** while　**4** by　**5** until　**6** ago　**7** during

E　Listen and tick the box.

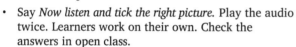

- Say *These questions are all about Sam's school trip to the science museum. You are going to hear Sam and his mother talking about it.*
- Give learners a minute to read the questions and look at the picture answers.
- Say *Now listen and tick the right picture.* Play the audio twice. Learners work on their own. Check the answers in open class.

26

Answers

1 A　**2** B　**3** C　**4** A　**5** C

Tapescript:

Listen and look. There is one example.

When will Sam arrive at the science museum?

Mum:　Sam, are you ready? It's five to nine!

Sam:　OK, Mum. Don't worry. What time will we get to the science museum? Nine thirty?

Mum:　No. You'll get there at a quarter past ten. It's quite a long journey.

Sam:　All right. Thanks.

Can you see the tick?

Now you listen and tick the box.

1　What does Sam hope to see at the museum?

Sam:　I hope it'll be fun there. I don't want to spend lots of time reading about medicine. I'm not interested in that.

Mum:　What are you interested in?

Sam:　The cat with seven toes!

Mum:　Oh!

Sam:　Yes. I hope we can go and see that before we walk around the spaceship there.

2　What hasn't Sam got in his bag yet?

Mum:　So, have you got everything?

Sam:　Well, I've found my sunglasses. They're in my bag.

Mum:　That's good. You'll need those. What about your tablet?

Sam:　I haven't put that in yet. But I haven't forgotten it, and I've got some money.

Mum:　Good.

3　What work will Sam take?

Sam:　I'm going to take some work with me.

Mum:　You mean math?

Sam:　That's right. I've already done my music homework.

Mum:　What about those geography questions?

Sam:　I found all the answers online. No problem.

4　Where will Sam have lunch?

Mum:　Where will your group have lunch? Outside?

Sam:　We won't do that. It's going to rain. And we can't go and sit in the café. There are too many kids in the group.

Mum:　So?

Sam:　Our teacher said there's a kind of classroom on the top floor. That's where we'll eat.

5　Who must Sam text before he goes?

Mum:　Please send me a text at midday, Sam. Have you got your phone?

Sam:　Yes, Mum. Actually, I have to text my friend Harry before I leave. I'll do that now.

Mum:　Oh.

Sam:　I want to sit next to him on the school bus. His father is our new science teacher!

Test tip: FLYERS
Listening (Part 4)

✔ Learners listen to a conversation and choose the correct picture (of three) that shows the right answer to a question. Before doing this task, train learners to carefully look at all three pictures and to look for differences between them.

→ Give learners sets of pictures that show, e.g. three animals, items of food, outfits, activities, and ask them to say what they see in each picture in pairs. (e.g. This is a beetle, an eagle and a swan. This is a yoghurt, these are olives and this is butter. Here, the girl is wearing a belt, and here, some trainers and here, some gloves.)

F　Ask one person different questions about their job. Then write their answers on the blue lines.

- Learners look at the pictures. Ask *Which jobs do these people do? Would you like to do any of these jobs? Which other jobs are you interested in? Why?* (learners answer) Other jobs on the Flyers word list are: *actor, astronaut, designer, engineer, journalist, manager, mechanic, singer* and *waiter*.
- In L1, tell learners to imagine they are going to interview one of the people in the picture (or another person doing a job of their own choice). Say *You are going to write about doing this job on your school website. You need some information, so think of five questions you would like to ask this person. Write your questions on the black dotted lines.*
- Learners choose a job and then work on their own or in pairs.

Suggestions: *What time do you start work? Do you have to wear special clothes? What part of your job is the most interesting / most dangerous? Did you want to do this job when you were a child? How many hours do you work each week? Do you work by yourself or in a team? Where do you do most of your work?*

- When learners have finished, different pairs ask two or three of their questions in open class. The class discusses what the answers might be. Accept answers in L1 if necessary.
- Learners then add answers on the blue dotted lines. Walk around and help with further ideas and/or vocabulary if necessary.

Which three lessons are Sam and Sarah in? Listen and tick the boxes.

- Learners look at the pictures. Ask *Which lessons do these pictures show?* (maths, geography, science, music, history)
- Say *We're going to listen to Sam and Sarah. They are talking during three of these lessons. Listen and tick the lessons.*
- Play the audio. Learners tick the boxes for the lessons that Sam and Sarah are in.

27

Answers
4 music, 5 history, 2 geography

Tapescript:

Sam:	Sarah? Which lesson have we got after the break? I can't remember.
Sarah:	Art. Did you do your homework?
Sam:	Yes. And hey … I know this tune, but what kind of instrument is this?
Sarah:	I'm not sure. We'll have to guess. Let's listen again, more carefully.
Sam:	OK.
Sarah:	Sam? Who invented telephones?
Sam:	Alexander Bell. Was that one of your science homework questions?
Sarah:	No! It's for the project that I'm doing at the moment – important things that happened during the nineteenth century.
Sam:	I've counted these three times. They still don't look right.
Sarah:	Let me look. I think there are seven different kinds of clouds, not six, Sam.
Sam:	Oh, OK. I'll open my first file and read that text again.

Look at the pictures. Write about the story. Write 20 or more words.

- Say *Look at the pictures. What happens in the story?* Learners suggest ideas. Learners then each write the story on their own. They can invent names and places and any other details. A good plan is to write two sentences about each picture in the present continuous tense.

- Ask different learners to read out their story.

Test tip: FLYERS
Reading and Writing (Part 7)

✔ Learners need to write a short story about what is happening in three pictures. Some learners might find this challenging at first.

→ Begin by asking learners to write three or four sentences about any single picture in the book. You could write questions on the board to help them: *Where are they? Why are they there? What are they doing now? What is going to happen next?* Learners work in groups to talk about possible answers before they write their final choice on a piece of paper. Collect all the answers and then read them out. Ask the class to guess which group wrote each set of answers. Learners will soon understand that a variety of answers are possible. This should increase their confidence.

Extension

The three pictures in Activity H can also be used as a prompt for Speaking Part 3 practice in another lesson, or as revision at the end of the course. Say *This story is called 'Lucy's bad day'. Lucy is late for school. While she's running, her pencil falls out of her bag.* In pairs, learners finish telling the story.

Complete the school alphabet poem.

- Revise the alphabet by reciting it chorally with learners. Learners then stand in a line with their names in alphabetical order. Ask each learner in the line *What letter does your name start with?*

- Learners look at Activity I. Ask *What's the poem about?* (school) Ask different learners to each read out a line in the first two verses.

- Divide the class into small groups. Say *Now you complete the poem for the other letters.* Learners work together to think of school words to complete the poem. Say *You can write more than one word for each letter if you want.*

- Groups read out their completed verse for the class. Choose one version and write it on the board. Learners then recite the whole poem in chorus. Read out the last line to congratulate learners on the completion of this level. Everyone could stand and clap and say *Good luck! Well done!* to their nearest classmate.

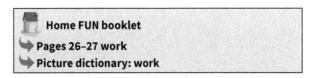

8 *Let's have fun!*

Make a scene from the story.

Learners look at page 71, Activity 8. Learners work
in pairs. Pairs choose the scene from the story they
would like to model. Give each pair an empty shoe
box. Learners then draw pictures of the classroom
walls. These should be the same size as the inside
faces of their shoe box. They glue these on the inside
of the shoe box. Then they can draw and cut out
people or classroom furniture and stick those to
the 'classroom floor' to create a 3D scene. Finally,
learners can cut out a window in one face of the box
to look through. Pairs then use their shoe box to
show and describe what is happening in this scene.

8 *Let's speak!*

Ask and answer about school.

Learners look at page 73, Activity 8. In pairs,
learners take turns to ask and answer the questions
about school. Different pairs tell the class about their
own or their partner's answers, e.g. *I go / I come /
She comes to school by bus. I sit / She sits next to Carla.
My/Her favourite lesson is history. I/She would like to
work in a museum.*

35

◀)) Let's say!

Say *Look at page 75, Activity 8. Listen.* Play the audio. Ask
*Did you hear the /ə/ sounds in dinner, mother, pizza, sugar,
butter, again, pictures, camera?* Say each word. Learners
repeat in chorus.
They could circle the /ə/ sounds on the page.
Learners listen to the rhyme again.
Say *Now you! You're getting better and better at this!*
Learners repeat the rhyme in chorus.
Say *There's an /ə/ sound in 'better' too. Can you hear it?*
Tell learners that this is the most common sound in
English.
Ask *Can you think of more story words with the sound /ə/
in them?* Learners find words in the story. Write their
suggestions on the board. (e.g. Sarah, teacher, different,
doctors, future, machine, invented, didn't, fingers,
journalists, managers, chocolate, remember, pepper,
together, over)
You could also show learners that *hour* and *our* sound
exactly the same.

Pirates!

Design the cover of your book.

This story is about a young pirate. She's called ....

....

....

....

....

2 Make the words

a	a	a	b	b	c
c	c	d	d	e	e
e	e	e	e	f	f
g	g	h	h	i	i
l	m	n	n	n	o
o	o	o	o	o	p
r	r	r	r	r	s
s	t	t	t	t	u
u	w	x	y	y	y

My town

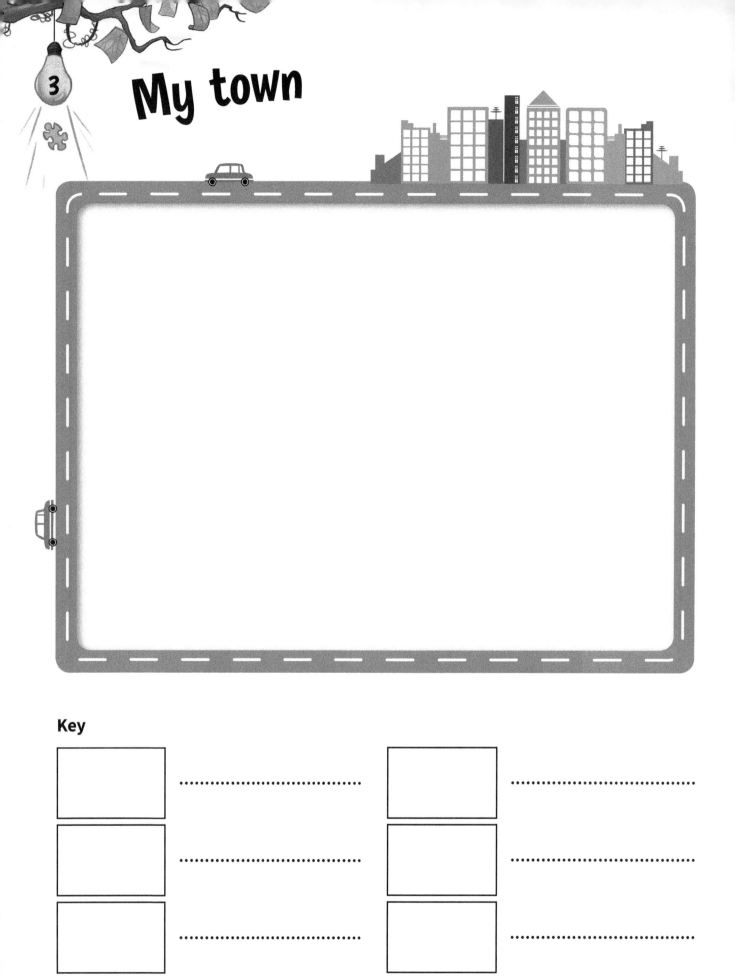

Key

My friend

My friend's face

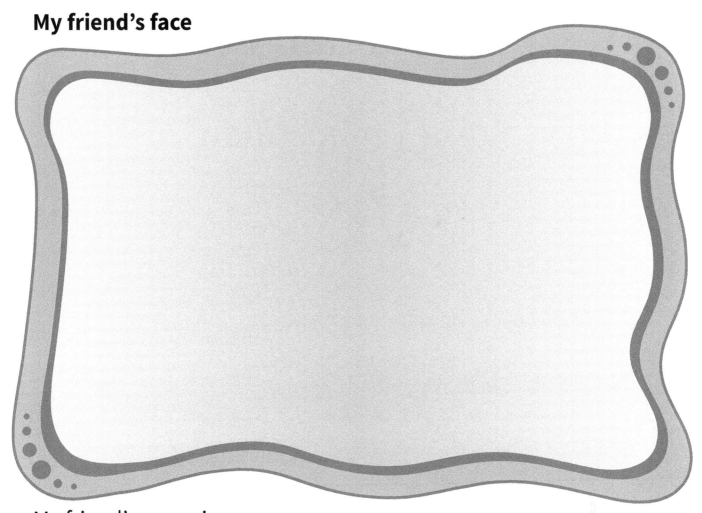

My friend's name is ....

My friend is .... years old.

My friend lives in ....

My friend's hobbies are ....

My friend's favourite thing in the world is ....

My friend hates ....

My friend loves ....

My friend's really good at ....!

My friend's really bad at ....!

My friend often says, '...'.

My friend never ....

Last weekend, my friend ....

I like my friend because ....

5 Stories

Story Competition

For children who are between 8 and .... years old.

Write a story about a ....

It must be .... words long!

Give it to Mrs .... in the school office.

Write your name and .... at the bottom of the page.

You must finish your story by Monday 12th ....

First prize is a ....

★ COME ON! ★
★ YOU CAN DO IT! ★

Did William do this?

Choose a word for each space.

for	on	off	off	over	~~up~~	up

Example: William didn't like getting ....up.............. in the morning.

1 William turned .... his mobile phone to see the time.

2 William fell .... near the school playground.

3 William took .... his shoes and put them in the spaceship.

4 William cut .... the space map.

5 William turned .... the computer in the spaceship.

6 William looked .... something that could help the alien.

We use this for ...

A

B

7

Travelling in time

Design your own time machine.

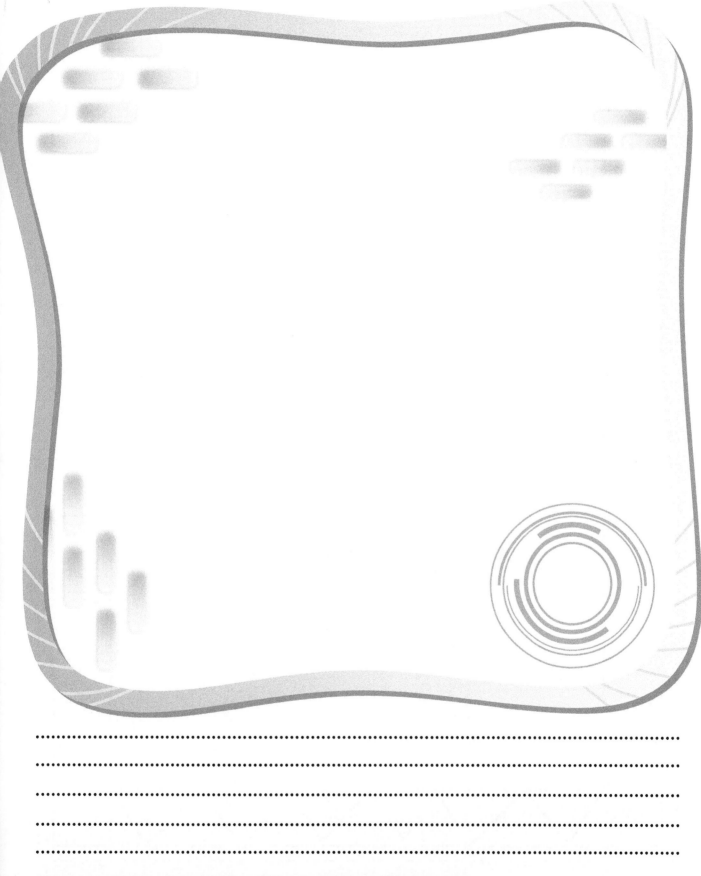

STORYFUN

6

To: ....

Name of school: ....

Date: ....

Signed: ....

Well done!

Audio track listing

Acknowledgements

The author would like to acknowledge the shared professionalism and FUN she's experienced whilst working with colleagues during 20 years of production of YLE tests. She would also like to thank CUP for their support in the writing of this second edition of *Storyfun*.

On a personal note, Karen fondly thanks her inspirational story-telling grandfather, and now, three generations later, her sons, Tom and Will, for adding so much creative fun to our continuation of the family story-telling and story-making tradition.

Design and typeset by Wild Apple Design.

Cover design and header artwork by Nicholas Jackson (Astound).

Sound recordings by Hart McLeod, Cambridge.

Music by Mark Fishlock and produced by Ian Harker. Recorded at The Soundhouse Studios, London.

The authors and publishers acknowledge the following sources of copyright material and are grateful for the permissions granted. While every effort has been made, it has not always been possible to identify the sources of all the material used, or to trace all copyright holders. If any omissions are brought to our notice, we will be happy to include the appropriate acknowledgements on reprinting.

The authors and publishers are grateful to the following illustrators:
Key: BL = Bottom Left; BR = Bottom Right; C = Centre; TC = Top Centre; TL = Top Left; TR = Top Right
Wild Apple Design pp. 54, 56, 57, 61
Mandy Field (Phosphor art) p. 59
Clive Goodyer p. 60
Harriet Stanes p. 62 (TL)
Sarah Warburton p. 62 (TC)
Alessia Trunfio (Astound) p. 62 (TR)
Sophie Allsopp p. 62 (C)
Giovanni Pota (Astound) p. 62 (BL)
Alan Brown (Advocate Art) p. 62 (BR)